WORK–LIFE
BALANCE

WORK–LIFE BALANCE

A practical guide for teachers

Margaret Adams

 David Fulton Publishers

David Fulton Publishers Ltd
The Chiswick Centre, 414 Chiswick High Road, London W4 5TF

www.fultonpublishers.co.uk

First published in Great Britain in 2006 by David Fulton Publishers

10 9 8 7 6 5 4 3 2 1

David Fulton Publishers is a division of Granada Learning Limited

British Library Cataloguing in Publication Data
A catalogue record for this book is available from the British Library.

ISBN: 1 84312 391 6

Typeset by RefineCatch Limited, Bungay, Suffolk
Printed and bound in Great Britain

Contents

Acknowledgements

With thanks to Anne Carter at Oxfordshire County Council for her continued interest in my approach to work–life balance in schools and to all the people in Berkshire schools who attended the Adams Consultancy Ltd's work–life balance programmes – in some cases more than once. Thanks also to the teachers and consultants who tried out the different versions of the work–life balance audit as it developed.

Above all, thanks to John Adams for his practical support throughout the time I have been working with the work–life balance agenda.

Margaret Adams
January 2006

Towards work–life balance

Welcome to this guide and self-help book for teachers on work–life balance. If you're struggling to find the time to flick through this book, let alone read it, this book is for you. If you are conscious of all the things you still have to do, today, this week, this term; if you are dissatisfied with your life because you never seem to have the opportunity to do the things you want to do; and if you are feeling guilty because you are compromising your personal life, your health and your relationships in order to complete tasks for school, or to fit everything that is important to you into your life, then this book is for you.

If you're thinking all of the above but also know that, despite everything, you want to stay in teaching, this book is *definitely* for you.

This book is about work–life balance – *your* work–life balance. It will help you to:

- understand what you mean by work–life balance
- find the right work–life balance for you
- know when you have achieved work–life balance.

As you use the book you will learn how to:

- manage your working life effectively in order to enable you to address work–life balance issues sensibly
- make the really important life planning decisions and to make sure they are the *right* decisions

- manage the interface between your working life and your life outside work differently, in ways which will help you to balance these major components of your life effectively
- be more aware of how the world of work is changing and how this affects you as a teacher
- take control of your life at work and in your life beyond work.

Finally, this book will help you to sustain sound work–life balance, because having worked hard to achieve work–life balance you need to make sure you don't lose it.

How to use this guide

This guide is divided into six sections. Each section addresses work–life balance from a different perspective. Most people will benefit from working through each of the sections in order, but you can use any section independently if you prefer.

There is a summary at the end of each section to remind you of the key points covered.

Each section includes activities to be completed as you read, or after you have worked through the section. These activities can be used as self-help and self-development exercises and as material to support staff development sessions on work–life balance in your school.

About the sections

Chapter 1: Why do teachers need guidance on work–life balance?

This section explains how, whether you realise it or not, some of the changes which have taken place in society are having an impact on your life and on your ability to achieve the right work–life balance for you as a teacher. It also explains why there is no single, universally accepted definition of work–life balance and invites you to think about what work–life balance means for you.

Use this section to give you an overview of the issues which are preventing teachers from achieving sound work–life balance, to refine your understanding of work–life balance and to begin to think about what achieving work–life balance means to you.

Chapter 2: The work–life balance audit

This section asks you to make a judgement about your current success in dealing with the major work–life balance issues. The section is presented in the form of a work–life balance audit.

Use the audit to help you to establish whether or not you have the right work–life balance at present, to help you to identify the areas of your life where you need to take action in order to improve your work–life balance and to test if you are sufficiently aware of the impact of the work–life balance agenda on schools.

Chapter 3: Work–life balance and work

This section focuses on you and your work. Getting things right at work is an essential part of achieving work–life balance. Since work takes up such a lot of your time it is a good place to begin the work–life balance journey.

Use this section to help you to establish how best to manage your working life, and to understand why teachers find it difficult to leave work behind when they go home, or in some cases to be able to switch off from work at all. Also use this section to help you to begin to take control of your working life.

Chapter 4: Life beyond work

This section is about how you plan and manage your whole life and how you manage the interface between your working life and your life outside work. It will help you to contain your working life within defined limits, to identify what's really important in your life, to be clear about the sort of work–life balance you want, and to establish the boundaries between your working life and the other components of your life.

Use this section to help you to be clear about what you want from your life, to help you with life planning and to help you to take the steps you need to ensure you lead the life you really want and achieve the right work–life balance for you.

Chapter 5: The new working environment

This section will help you to become more aware of recent developments in the world of work which will help you to achieve your work–life balance aspirations. It also offers you guidance on how to approach your head teacher about changing some of your school's working practices to help create an environment that is more likely to promote sound work–life balance for everyone in the school.

Use this section to assist you to place your work–life balance aspirations in the working context and to establish exactly how recent developments in working practices and employment options can help you on your work–life balance journey.

Chapter 6: Can you achieve work–life balance and stay in teaching?

If you have reached this point in the guide you already know the answer to the question. This section will help you to recap on what you have learned, and as you do so, to see how using that advice will continue to help you on your work–life balance journey. The section also contains guidance to help you to sustain your work–life balance once you have achieved it.

Use this section to confirm what you are doing well and to keep on track as far as your work–life balance is concerned in the future.

CHAPTER 1

Why do teachers need guidance on work–life balance?

Overview

This section of the guide will help you to be more aware of why teachers need help to achieve the work–life balance they are looking for. It also considers what work–life balance means and what teachers need to do as they begin their work–life balance journey.

Introduction

Work–life balance is a fairly new term and yet the need to balance the demands of working life with the demands of life outside work in order to lead a satisfying life has always been with us. Teachers, like all professional people, have always had a lot to do, but over the years they seem to have managed reasonably well without guidance on work–life balance. People have always had to make decisions about what they can fit into their lives and how to manage conflicting demands, whether at work or in their lives outside work, and they seem to have done so without help to manage this.

So, here in the twenty-first century, why do you need guidance on work–life balance? The simple answer is that the changes which are taking place in the world of work make it more difficult for everyone in work to achieve sound work–life balance. More and more people are struggling to prevent work from swamping their lives. They need help if they are going to establish what type of work–life balance they want and to find ways of achieving the right balance for them.

You're probably reading this guide because you think the same.

Changing times

Most of us, whether or not we are teachers, are aware that we live in a 24–7, 365 days-a-year, fast-moving economy. As users of services today we expect:

- services to be delivered on demand
- service quality to be improving constantly.

With the advent of new and ever-improving technology we also expect faster responses to enquiries and speedy action when we request activity from service providers, whether they are in the public or the private sector. We expect to be able to shop at any time of the day or night and to travel, transact and complete business and leisure activities anywhere, anytime. We demand same-day replies by e-mail where once an exchange of letters could have taken a week.

We are also beginning to expect our interactions with the public sector to reflect our experiences with businesses. We want to have our NHS x-rays and scans at the weekend, early in the morning or in the evening. We would like to visit the local library on Sundays and, with the advent of e-government, we expect to be able to view our neighbours' planning applications on-line, any time.

As with the rest of the world, the educational world moves faster today than ever before. The demand for speed and immediacy of response drives education professionals just as these same expectations drive other parts of society. As a teacher you are no doubt aware of increased pressures on you to complete tasks quickly when dealing with parents, your LEA, the inspectorates and a range of other groups, including members of the public.

The demands for change do not stop there. As consumers and service users we also expect to see regular improvements to service quality. Not only do we expect services to be delivered quickly, we also expect services to be delivered to higher and higher standards. As a consequence, what was perceived to be good performance yesterday is only satisfactory today and will be unsatisfactory tomorrow.

These changes do not leave education untouched. As teachers everywhere know, raising standards is a key objective for education's professionals.

Workforce reform, curricular reform and innovation, changes to Ofsted requirements, and so on, all bring change to teachers' ways of working as they seek to raise standards. Thus, there is more pressure today on everyone at work:

- to work faster
- to be speedily responsive to the demands of service users
- to complete tasks to tighter and tighter deadlines
- to raise standards of service delivery.

As a teacher you will be aware of these pressures. As you try to deal with them you have probably found that work itself has expanded. There just isn't time to complete work in defined working hours or in a 'normal' working day, so work takes up more and more of your life.

More work is now completed in time that once belonged to your life outside work. Home becomes just another workplace and work fills your waking hours. Work usurps the place of leisure and much-needed exercise, damages relationships and creates situations where you just cannot forget work and relax. Even when watching television the e-mails and the laptop call.

Work today is more likely than ever before to swamp your whole life. So there is a need – and that need is growing – to help teachers struggling with all these demands to find ways:

- to prevent work from taking over their lives
- to regain control if work has become all-consuming
- to lead a satisfying life.

Thus there is a need to give more attention to the concept of work–life balance, now.

But has anything really changed?

Some people will argue that this is nothing new. Professional groups have always eschewed a defined working week, working until the job is completed without reference to the clock. They have worked in their own time to keep their skills up to date and have often gained real pleasure from what they do. In such circumstances, it has been argued, work is a pleasure and as much a relaxation as any leisure activity. To contemplate preventing teachers from 'working' in this context would seem to be a nonsense. It would also be a move that many teachers would oppose.

Today, however, more and more teachers need to work outside the 'normal' working day in order to meet the next day's deadlines. They are no longer working long hours because of their love of their subject or because of a desire to help learners; they are struggling to keep up with the growing demands of the job. They are working under increasing pressure, driven both by their own desires to do a good job and by the expectations of others to perform and to achieve. Taking work home and working a substantial number of hours at home in addition to working full-time in school has become the norm for many teachers.

These same teachers do not know how to redress the situation, even though they know that the quality of their lives and their relationships is suffering as a result of their approach to their work. They have poor work–life balance and do not know how to improve it.

Activity 1.1, which you will find at the end of the chapter, will help you to take stock of the ways in which you manage your working life at present. Complete the activity now if you would like to reflect on your approach to your working life immediately. Complete it when you have finished reading the section if you would prefer to do all the activities together.

Why does work–life balance matter?

The foregoing may be true but does work–life balance really matter?

Yes, it does. Work–life balance matters in a very practical sense because the lack of it can lead to enormous problems both for individual teachers and for schools. Poor work–life balance is often seen as the result of working longer and longer hours and extending the working week at the expense of all other activities. There is plenty of evidence from organisations such as the Health and Safety Executive (HSE) to suggest that excessive working hours lead to:

- increased work-related stress
- lower overall productivity
- more accidents
- more long-term ill health.

All of these outcomes are bad news for education as well as for individual teachers.

Recent attempts to curb the maximum number of hours people work via the Working Time Directive have not been introduced for altruistic reasons. They aim, among other things, to improve worker safety and to reduce work-related stress which is a real problem in the modern workforce, especially in managerial and professional groups. According to the HSE, about half a million people in the UK experience work-related stress at a level they believe is making them ill. Up to five million people in the UK feel 'very' or 'extremely' stressed by their work, and work-related stress costs society billions of pounds every year.

So, work–life balance really matters.

Work–life balance also matters because work is only one part of life. To concentrate on work to the exclusion of other issues, and especially health, leisure, relationships, and responsibilities and interests outside work, risks causing problems for teachers and their schools, sooner or later. For example, there are plenty of people who have succeeded in their jobs, in education and elsewhere, at the expense of their health and their relationships with their partners or children. Many of these people regret the choices they have made when it is too late to do anything about them – when their health has gone and when their families have found that not only can they cope without the support of the person who always puts the job first, but they also prefer things that way.

When they are in senior positions – for example as head teachers – these people often seek to impose their values and their working style on their staff, thus perpetuating their approach. In such circumstances, those who do not fit in with the head teacher's preferred ways of working are made to feel guilty or that they lack commitment. Ultimately, staff and the school suffer.

Work–life balance also matters because the belief that teachers cannot achieve work–life balance sends a negative message to the public about the teaching profession. This is likely to have an adverse impact on teacher recruitment and retention. Some people already avoid a teaching career, or they choose not to stay in teaching, because of the working conditions. They are acutely aware of the expectation to work long hours and of the resulting poor quality of life they believe they must endure. They believe teaching is stressful, that the work is onerous, that the hours are long and the rewards, both financial and other, are poor. Thus they leave teaching or choose not to become teachers in the first place. This inevitably leads to heavier workloads and to impaired work–life balance for those who remain.

Work–life balance also matters because many people in the workforce today want to do other things with their lives apart from work. They have more diverse expectations concerning their working lives than people had in the recent past. Many people today do not want to work such long hours that they have no time or energy for activities other than work. They want jobs that will accommodate these changing aspirations.

It is not just younger teachers who want a different work–life balance. People at all stages in their lives are looking for better work–life balance.

The prospect of working until the age of 65, with fewer opportunities for early retirement, becomes daunting for any teacher if the job is one which drives everything but work out of a teacher's life. Therefore people of all ages are looking to create a different relationship between their working lives and their lives outside work.

Activity 1.2, which you will find at the end of the chapter, looks at the relationship between your working life and your life outside work. Completing this activity will give you an indication of some of the issues you will need to bear in mind as you work through this guide. Work on the activity now if you would like to reflect on these issues immediately. Complete it when you have finished reading the section if you would prefer to do all the activities together.

I SEEM TO HAVE LOST MY BALANCE

What is work–life balance?

Work–life balance is difficult to define because it is essentially a subjective concept. There is nothing fixed and stable about work–life balance and there is no fixed and generally accepted definition, although it is probably worth noting that individuals and employers tend to define it very differently.

For individuals, work–life balance is about achieving their personal goals both in their working lives and in their lives outside work. When people think about work–life balance, naturally enough they focus on their personal circumstances and on their whole lives, not just their working lives. Individuals arrive at their own judgements as to whether or not they have achieved the right balance for them. No-one can tell anyone else that he or she has achieved good or even satisfactory work–life balance.

Individuals build their understanding of work–life balance around their responses to two key questions:

- What sort of life do I want to lead? and
- What will I be doing in the various compartments of my life (work, family, recreation etc.) when I have achieved the right work–life balance for me?

This approach can present problems as most people find it easier to be aware of when they do not have the right work–life balance than to define what good work–life balance means for them or to be confident enough about their achievements to recognise good work–life balance when they have achieved it.

Work–life balance is a difficult concept for employers. When employers in both the public and the private sector talk about work–life balance they usually define it in terms of the people management strategies, policies and practices they introduce in order to support their employees.

For many employers work–life balance is about the introduction and management of a range of different ways of organising work to help to improve individual and organisational productivity and to improve staff morale (see Chapter 5). It may also be about making sure that people do not work more than 48 hours per week or do not average more than 48 hours' work per week over a defined period.

Employers cannot easily measure their employees' feelings or build up detailed knowledge of the issues their staff deal with in their lives beyond work, both of which are crucial to success with work–life balance, so they tend to judge success in achieving work–life balance in terms of:

- the impact of the changes they make to the organisation and management of work
- improvements to organisational performance
- the success of employee wellbeing programmes.

They then often equate these successes with success in terms of helping people to achieve work–life balance.

However, employers set up situations at work which then enable people to achieve sound work–life balance. They do not *create* work–life balance for people; people do that for themselves.

As a result of these different perceptions it is very easy to talk at cross-purposes about work–life balance.

Are work–life balance and wellbeing the same things?

Not really; they are different concepts and should not be confused.

Most guides on wellbeing cover issues related to health and the concept of wellness. The concepts are usually reviewed from the perspective of the employer and focus on the very laudable objectives of helping people to stay well, to avoid illness and to live healthy lives.

Supporting people in this way will help to set up an environment in which they may be more likely to achieve work–life balance but, in themselves, wellbeing initiatives do not ensure that people achieve the work–life balance they are looking for. However, people who work in organisations which take wellness and employee wellbeing seriously are likely to stand a better chance of achieving sound work–life balance.

What do teachers need to do to achieve good work–life balance?

Take heart. Working through this guide will help.

- The most pressing task for you as a teacher is to make sure that you take control of your life.

You will begin to do this by working though Chapters 2, 3 and 4. By doing that you will:

- establish how effectively you are currently managing your work–life balance
- develop your understanding of what work–life balance means
- develop your understanding of what you want to achieve at work and in your life outside work
- learn how to establish where you want to set the boundaries between your working life and the rest of your life.

Activity 1.3 deals with your current understanding of work–life balance, and completing it will help you to begin to plan your journey towards your work–life balance destination.

Now that you have finished reading this chapter complete this and any of the other activities linked to this section you have not yet considered.

Summary – key points

1   There is growing interest in work–life balance because more people today, including teachers, are struggling to prevent work from swamping their lives.

2   Many of the work–life balance problems people in work face stem from the changes that are taking place in the world of work.

3   People, including teachers, have changing expectations about their working lives and the relationship between their working lives and their lives outside work. They do not want to work such long hours that they have no time for activities other than work.

4   Many teachers find that the job is expanding and making additional demands on them. They struggle to cope, but one of the casualties in the struggle is often their work–life balance.

5   Poor work–life balance can lead to difficulties for individual teachers and for their schools.

6   There is no fixed and generally accepted definition of work–life balance.

7   For individuals, work–life balance is about achieving personal outcomes both in their working lives and in their lives outside work.

8   Employers usually define work–life balance in terms of the people management strategies, policies and practices they introduce in order to support their employees and to help them to improve their performance.

9   In order to improve their work–life balance, teachers need to take control of their lives.

Activities

After completing these activities make sure you keep the information you record safely. Review your responses as you prepare to work on Chapter 6.

Activities 1.1 and 1.2 are particularly suitable for school-based staff development sessions.

ACTIVITY 1.1: ANALYSING THE PRESENT (1)

Think about your own job and write down your answers to the following questions on a separate sheet of paper:

- How many hours do you work in a normal working week? Is this more hours than you think you should work? If it is, typically, how many extra hours over and above what you think you should be working do you give to the job each week?

- If you are working about the right number of hours, are there pressures on you to do more?

- When did you last rush to meet a deadline?

- How often in the last term have you had to do things so fast or respond so quickly that you have worried about the quality of your work?

- Do you take it for granted that you will be taking work home at the weekends?

- How often do you find you have to do tasks that are strictly not your job because there is no-one else to do them?

- How much of your time do you spend 'plugging the gaps' left because a post in your school has not been filled, because someone with a particular responsibility is absent or because there is no-one else to do the job?

- How often do you take on tasks 'just for the moment', until the school finds someone else to do them?

- Do you feel that your work has taken over your life?

- Overall, do you believe you are in control of your life?

ACTIVITY 1.2: ANALYSING THE PRESENT (2)

Think about your own job. Circle the most relevant response to the following questions:

● Do you achieve everything you need to achieve?

always   usually   often   sometimes   never

● Do you achieve everything you want to achieve?

always   usually   often   sometimes   never

● Whatever age you are now, do you think you will want to work in the way you do now until you are 65?

Think about your life outside work.

● Do you know how many hours you allocate to your life outside work in a typical week?

● Do you achieve everything you need to achieve?

always   usually   often   sometimes   never

● Do you achieve everything you want to achieve?

always   usually   often   sometimes   never

Review your answers, then consider the following:

● If you find you cannot fit everything you would like to do into your life at work and your life outside work, what sort of activities are likely to be squeezed out? Prioritise the list which follows. Put a 1 beside the activity which is most likely to be lost, a 2 beside the next most likely, etc.

adequate marking and preparation activities

exercise

healthy eating

relaxation

interests and hobbies

time with your family, your partner, children etc.

time spent with your extended family and/or friends, e.g. social occasions/events

jobs around the house/garden – car fixing/general maintenance etc.

ACTIVITY 1.3: WORK–LIFE BALANCE AND YOU

Having read Chapter 1, which of the statements about work–life balance contained in that chapter seem most relevant to you? Write down your thoughts.

What have you learned about work–life balance from this chapter that will help you to achieve or sustain the right work–life balance for you?

Note here your definition of work–life balance. Be prepared to revise this as you work through the rest of this guide.

What are the implications of this chapter for your personal work–life balance?

What is the first thing you need to do to help you to achieve or sustain the work–life balance that is right for you?

CHAPTER 2

The work–life balance audit

Overview

This section of the guide will help you to establish where you are now with regard to achieving the right work–life balance for you. It will help you to be more aware of some of the issues and situations where behaving differently could help you to improve your work–life balance. It will also help you to be more aware of the issues you need to address in order to achieve the right work–life balance for you.

About the audit

There are two work–life balance audits in this section. The full work–life balance audit comprises 50 multiple-choice questions. The quick audit contains 25 questions.

If you like audits and self-assessments then follow the instructions below and work through all 50 questions of the full audit. Take as much time as you like to complete the activity. You are likely to need a minimum of 20 minutes.

If you would prefer just to get an overview of where you stand with regard to work–life balance, then complete the quick audit, which comprises the first 25 questions of the full audit. Again, take as much time as you like, but you will probably need at least ten minutes.

Completing the audit

Turn to page 27 where you will find grids on which to record your responses. Either remove the page for the relevant audit or photocopy it. Use the grid headed 'First Attempt' as you work through the audit.

Whether you are completing the full audit or the quick audit, in each case you should choose a single answer from the list of alternatives given and record a tick against answer a, b or c in the relevant box. If you do not think that any of the answers exactly fits your response, choose the answer which is closest to the one you would like to make.

When you have finished the audit, review your score in line with the guidance which you will find later in this section.

The work–life balance audit

Start here, whether you are completing the full audit or the quick audit.

1 Does your school have a work–life balance policy?

   a Yes

   b No

   c No, but one is under consideration

2 Do you have guaranteed non-contact time each week?

   a No

   b Yes, I mean, well – sometimes

   c Yes, I know that I have time I can count on each week

3 What do you do when you have too much to do and too many calls on your time?

   a Try to do everything, and so some things badly

   b Concentrate on the important things and let the others go

   c Do the things that people shout loudest to have done

4 'Flexible working – that is varying working hours and patterns of attendance in order to help employees manage their work and their lives outside work more effectively – is more popular in the private sector than in the public sector.' Is this statement true or false?

   a True

   b False

5 On a day when everyone in school seems to be busy, several people are asking you to help them. Given that you cannot help everyone, in which order should you accept additional tasks?

   1 Tasks I like doing
   2 Tasks that only I can do
   3 Any tasks linked to my job
   4 Tasks where the deadline for completion is earliest

   a 1, 2, 3, 4

   b 2, 3, 4, 1

   c 2, 4, 1, 3

6 Do you often wake up in the night, thinking about work?

   a Yes

   b No

7 Which of the following, under the terms of the Employment Act 2002, have the legal right to ask to work flexibly and to have their requests considered seriously?

   a Every employee

   b Employees responsible for the upbringing of children

   c Employees responsible for the upbringing of children under the age of six

8 If you are asked to attend a meeting after school that will not be dealing with an area of your responsibility do you:

   a Decline to attend immediately

b Attend and think about your own work during the meeting

c Say you will attend and then find an emergency or crisis to prevent you from getting there

9 'A state of complete physical, mental and social wellbeing' is, according to the World Health Organisation, a definition of:

a work–life balance

b wellbeing

c health

10 How high a profile does work–life balance have in your school?

a We never discuss work–life balance

b It is an agenda item at all staff meetings

c People raise the subject occasionally

11 A senior person in school asks you to take charge of the teaching resource bank which is disorganised and overloaded. In order to make the resource area useful to everyone do you:

a Buy more filing cabinets

b Ask people to make a bit of space in their storage areas

c Draw up guidelines for storage and the archiving of relevant, current material and ask people to throw away everything else

12 Which organisation has produced a set of management standards for dealing with stress at work?

a Department for Education and Skills

b Institute of Public Policy Research

c Health and Safety Executive

13 Do you have hobbies and interests outside your work?

a Yes

b No

14 How often do you allocate a quiet time somewhere in your schedule (before school, after school, in non-contact time etc.) when you can reflect on your priorities?

   a At least once a week

   b About once a month

   c I never have time to be quiet

15 You are having an after-school department/key stage/pastoral meeting and one of the teachers has brought in some snacks which he or she forces on you. Do you feel guilty if you throw the food away because you don't like it?

   a Yes.

   b No

16 Does your school ensure that information about work–life balance and what the school is doing to help staff to achieve sound work–life balance is effectively communicated to everyone?

   a Yes

   b No

17 You have been looking for an important e-mail but can't find it. As you search for it you discover that you have over a thousand e-mails in your in-box. What do you do?

   a Say that's why you asked for a new laptop/hard drive

   b File the relevant ones in subject folders, delete the rest, and start again

   c Delete the lot and start again

18 You have decided to spend an afternoon during half-term just relaxing and doing not very much. A teacher who used to work in your school, but with whom you were never particularly friendly, telephones and suggests you meet up. You are not very keen on the idea. What do you do?

   a Agree to the meeting because you don't like disappointing people b Say no, but feel guilty about refusing all afternoon

c Say you have a prior commitment and enjoy your afternoon as planned

19 You regularly spend Thursday evenings with friends at a local pub, but for some time you haven't been enjoying your visits. Do you:

a Stop going, giving the real reason if your friends ask

b Say that the evenings are starting to be a bit expensive so you won't be coming as often in the future

c Carry on as before; you don't have anything better to do on Thursdays anyway

20 How aware would you say senior staff in your school are about developments in the area of flexible working, including recent legislation on this subject?

a Very aware

b Quite aware

c Not aware

21 Are all of the following causes of work-related stress?

- Heavy workloads
- Long and unsocial working hours
- Lack of control over the job
- Lack of appropriate training
- The perception that the job done has no value or worth

a Yes

b No

22 If your head teacher told the staff that the new working arrangements he or she was introducing would ensure you all achieve work–life balance, which of the following responses would best indicate that you have a good understanding of work–life balance?

a Only I know when I have achieved work–life balance. The head is not in a position to tell me b I'm glad the head is making the decision for me. I've no idea what work–life balance is

c We ought to have a meeting to agree what work–life balance is; then everyone will know what they should be doing

23 In 2003–4, according to the Health and Safety Executive, how many working days were lost in the United Kingdom due to stress?

a Almost 10 million

b Almost 13 million

c Almost 16 million

24 Discretionary time is the term used to describe time you can use in any way you think fit. Do you have enough discretionary time in your life?

a Yes

b No

25 If a teacher in school told you that he or she is taking up a flexible working option, is that teacher necessarily opting to work part-time?

a Yes

b No

If you are completing the quick audit go to the scoring information at the end of the questions now.

---

26 Since the introduction of recent legislation, which of the following statements is unlikely to be construed to be a legitimate reason for refusing an employee's request to work flexibly?

a We won't be able to find additional staff to do your job

b We need everyone on the premises at the start of the school day

c We won't be able to meet parents' needs

27 How often do you work right through lunchtimes at school?

   a Most days

   b About once a week

   c Once a month or less

28 Look at the three lists of items which should be included in a job description noted below. Which list includes an item which is not normally found in job descriptions?

   a Job purpose, key results areas, job activities/tasks

   b Job purpose, job activities/tasks, required job knowledge

   c Job purpose, role holder's salary, key results areas

29 The prime purpose of health and wellbeing programmes is:

   a To help people improve their work–life balance

   b To prevent illness and injury and to promote good health among all staff

   c To help people who are not coping

30 'The Working Time Regulations, introduced into the United Kingdom in 1998, were introduced primarily as a health and safety measure.' Is this statement true or false?

   a True

   b False

31 What support does your school offer to members of your staff who have children of their own?

   a We don't do anything specific to support this group

   b We hold information about local childcare services at a central point in the office and have a list of contacts

   c We have a parents' support group (for our staff who are also parents) and provide facilities for regular meetings

32 If a school has a problem with 'presenteeism' it has difficulties with:

   a Getting learners to come to school

   b Staff absence

   c Getting staff to focus on achievements rather than on the hours they spend in school

33 Which of the following statements would be the closest to the response you think you would receive from a head teacher committed to helping you to achieve sound work–life balance if you asked to work at home for part of the working week?

   a Let's see which parts of your job you could do at home

   b Home working is what you do when school is closed. It's called working late and at the weekends

   c I don't think you should be working at home

34 Which indicates the better use of time?

   a Doing the right thing

   b Doing things right

35 Which of the following is the most important document in helping you to get control of your working life?

   a Your job description

   b Your school's work–life balance policy

   c Recent legislation/directives about working hours etc.

36 Recently published statistics state that more than 25 per cent of the working population currently works more than 48 hours per week. What would be the situation in a school which takes work–life balance seriously?

   a No-one works more than 48 hours per week

   b We all work long hours; that's life in education

   c People work the hours they want to; if they want to work long hours that's their choice

37 How do you respond when you come to consider throwing something away that isn't life-expired?

    a I don't do it. I keep things just in case

    b Very guilty! I do get rid of things sometimes but it's a wrench

    c It's no use to me anymore, so it has to go

38 You are thinking of taking a job in a new school and need to know about housing costs in the area before accepting a job. Which of the following is closest to the reply a head who values his or her staff is likely to make to your enquiry?

    a Let's discuss what sort of property you would be looking for and I'll arrange for you to talk to our two local estate agents

    b I know housing costs around here are quite high but that's about all I can tell you. I bought my house a long time ago

    c I think we might have some estate agents' literature somewhere in school. I'll try to find it for you

39 You want to take up a new activity (e.g. learn a foreign language, learn how to ride, take a cookery class etc.) but just can't fit it into your current schedule. What do you say?

    a I'll have time for it, one day, maybe when I retire

    b I'll stop doing something I do at present to make room

    c It's not fair; why can't I do what I want with my life?

40 What is your school doing to help staff to avoid work-related stress?

    a Training managers to understand their health and safety responsibilities

    b Conducting health and safety risk assessments which deal with work-related stress

    c Both a and b

41 Several teachers in school intend to take up their extended leave entitlements (maternity leave, paternity leave, adoption leave etc.). Which of the statements below do you think would be nearest to

the reaction of a head teacher committed to helping his or her staff to achieve sound work–life balance?

a I would ask them to try to come back sooner rather than later because the children will suffer as a result of their prolonged absence

b I would accept their decisions, assure them we will deal with the situation and tell them not to be concerned about school issues while they are on leave

c I would question their loyalty to the school in making such a choice

42 You have been working at home for two days on an important document and were expected to call your head at a particular time yesterday. You were working on the project all day but forgot to telephone. Unfortunately that day was also the day when a sport which your head knows you follow was on television. When you go back into school your head asks you about the telephone call. What would you say?

a I tried to ring you but the lines were busy both times I called

b Sorry, I forgot, but the work is done

c Sorry, I forgot, and before you ask, I wasn't watching the match

43 According to central government how many people will be caring for elderly relatives by 2010?

a 10 million

b 15 million

c 20 million

44 During your appraisal your manager asks you how you manage to avoid distractions when you are working in the staff room. Which of the following is closest to your response?

a I yell at people if they interrupt me when I'm working

b I usually break off and accept that I'm not going to get anything done c I decide beforehand what I need to get done and tell people that I am working if they interrupt me while I am doing those things

45 Do you find that your work takes up so much of your time that you do not have enough time for your hobbies, interests and social activities?

a Yes

b No

46 On a day when you are particularly busy a colleague asks you to take on an extra task. The first question you should ask yourself before taking on that task is:

a Does the job need to be done?

b Can I do this job?

c Whose responsibility is the job?

47 You have planned a weekend away and have told your head teacher you will be leaving school promptly on Friday afternoon in order to get to the airport. As you are about to leave school the head asks you to check some statistics in a report. He says it will only take a minute. You know it will take at least 15 minutes. You do not have 15 minutes to spare. What would you do?

a Check the statistics and hope you can get through the check-in quickly

b Say that you will check the figures on Monday

c Take the document with you and work on the statistics during your weekend away

48 An opportunity cost is:

a The price you pay for turning down a promotion

b The time and energy you have to put into a task to make it a success

c The costs in terms of what you cannot do once you make a choice to use your time in a particular way

49 If you worked in a school where the head teacher was committed to helping the staff to achieve sound work–life balance and you said to him or her that as a result of too heavy a workload your health is being damaged, do you think your head would:

a Promise to look into your situation when he or she has time

b Remove some of the tasks from your job

c Tell you that the workload comes with the job; after all, you're a teacher!

50 And finally, which of the following sums up your feelings about your own work–life balance?

a I have achieved the right work–life balance for me

b One day I'll think about work–life balance; for the moment I've too much else to do

c I have made some changes to the way I work, but I need to do more

Recording your score – quick audit

Tick your response

	First Attempt				Second Attempt			
1a ❏	11a ❏	21a ❏		1a ❏	11a ❏	21a ❏
1b ❏	11b ❏	21b ❏		1b ❏	11b ❏	21b ❏
1c ❏	11c ❏	22a ❏		1c ❏	11c ❏	22a ❏
2a ❏	12a ❏	22b ❏		2a ❏	12a ❏	22b ❏
2b ❏	12b ❏	22c ❏		2b ❏	12b ❏	22c ❏
2c ❏	12c ❏	23a ❏		2c ❏	12c ❏	23a ❏
3a ❏	13a ❏	23b ❏		3a ❏	13a ❏	23b ❏
3b ❏	13b ❏	23c ❏		3b ❏	13b ❏	23c ❏
3c ❏	14a ❏	24a ❏		3c ❏	14a ❏	24a ❏
4a ❏	14b ❏	24b ❏		4a ❏	14b ❏	24b ❏
4b ❏	14c ❏	25a ❏		4b ❏	14c ❏	25a ❏
5a ❏	15a ❏	25b ❏		5a ❏	15a ❏	25b ❏
5b ❏	15b ❏			5b ❏	15b ❏
5c ❏	16a ❏			5c ❏	16a ❏
6a ❏	16b ❏			6a ❏	16b ❏
6b ❏	17a ❏			6b ❏	17a ❏
7a ❏	17b ❏			7a ❏	17b ❏
7b ❏	17c ❏			7b ❏	17c ❏
7c ❏	18a ❏			7c ❏	18a ❏
8a ❏	18b ❏			8a ❏	18b ❏
8b ❏	18c ❏			8b ❏	18c ❏
8c ❏	19a ❏			8c ❏	19a ❏
9a ❏	19b ❏			9a ❏	19b ❏
9b ❏	19c ❏			9b ❏	19c ❏
9c ❏	20a ❏			9c ❏	20a ❏
10a ❏	20b ❏			10a ❏	20b ❏
10b ❏	20c ❏			10b ❏	20c ❏
10c ❏				10c ❏

Note your score below

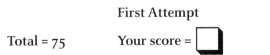

	First Attempt	Second Attempt
Total = 75	Your score = ☐	Your Score = ☐

Recording your score – full audit

Tick your response

First Attempt

1a ☐	11a ☐	21a ☐	31a ☐	41a ☐
1b ☐	11b ☐	21b ☐	31b ☐	41b ☐
1c ☐	11c ☐	22a ☐	31c ☐	41c ☐
2a ☐	12a ☐	22b ☐	32a ☐	42a ☐
2b ☐	12b ☐	22c ☐	32b ☐	42b ☐
2c ☐	12c ☐	23a ☐	32c ☐	42c ☐
3a ☐	13a ☐	23b ☐	33a ☐	43a ☐
3b ☐	13b ☐	23c ☐	33b ☐	43b ☐
3c ☐	14a ☐	24a ☐	33c ☐	43c ☐
4a ☐	14b ☐	24b ☐	34a ☐	44a ☐
4b ☐	14c ☐	25a ☐	34b ☐	44b ☐
5a ☐	15a ☐	25b ☐	35a ☐	44c ☐
5b ☐	15b ☐	26a ☐	35b ☐	45a ☐
5c ☐	16a ☐	26b ☐	35c ☐	45b ☐
6a ☐	16b ☐	26c ☐	36a ☐	46a ☐
6b ☐	17a ☐	27a ☐	36b ☐	46b ☐
7a ☐	17b ☐	27b ☐	36c ☐	46c ☐
7b ☐	17c ☐	27c ☐	37a ☐	47a ☐
7c ☐	18a ☐	28a ☐	37b ☐	47b ☐
8a ☐	18b ☐	28b ☐	37c ☐	47c ☐
8b ☐	18c ☐	28c ☐	38a ☐	48a ☐
8c ☐	19a ☐	29a ☐	38b ☐	48b ☐
9a ☐	19b ☐	29b ☐	38c ☐	48c ☐
9b ☐	19c ☐	29c ☐	39a ☐	49a ☐
9c ☐	20a ☐	30a ☐	39b ☐	49b ☐
10a ☐	20b ☐	30b ☐	39c ☐	49c ☐
10b ☐	20c ☐		40a ☐	50a ☐
10c ☐			40b ☐	50b ☐
			40c ☐	50c ☐

Note your score below

Total = 150   Your score = ☐

Recording your score – full audit

Tick your response

Second Attempt

1a ❏	11a ❏	21a ❏	31a ❏	41a ❏
1b ❏	11b ❏	21b ❏	31b ❏	41b ❏
1c ❏	11c ❏	22a ❏	31c ❏	41c ❏
2a ❏	12a ❏	22b ❏	32a ❏	42a ❏
2b ❏	12b ❏	22c ❏	32b ❏	42b ❏
2c ❏	12c ❏	23a ❏	32c ❏	42c ❏
3a ❏	13a ❏	23b ❏	33a ❏	43a ❏
3b ❏	13b ❏	23c ❏	33b ❏	43b ❏
3c ❏	14a ❏	24a ❏	33c ❏	43c ❏
4a ❏	14b ❏	24b ❏	34a ❏	44a ❏
4b ❏	14c ❏	25a ❏	34b ❏	44b ❏
5a ❏	15a ❏	25b ❏	35a ❏	44c ❏
5b ❏	15b ❏	26a ❏	35b ❏	45a ❏
5c ❏	16a ❏	26b ❏	35c ❏	45b ❏
6a ❏	16b ❏	26c ❏	36a ❏	46a ❏
6b ❏	17a ❏	27a ❏	36b ❏	46b ❏
7a ❏	17b ❏	27b ❏	36c ❏	46c ❏
7b ❏	17c ❏	27c ❏	37a ❏	47a ❏
7c ❏	18a ❏	28a ❏	37b ❏	47b ❏
8a ❏	18b ❏	28b ❏	37c ❏	47c ❏
8b ❏	18c ❏	28c ❏	38a ❏	48a ❏
8c ❏	19a ❏	29a ❏	38b ❏	48b ❏
9a ❏	19b ❏	29b ❏	38c ❏	48c ❏
9b ❏	19c ❏	29c ❏	39a ❏	49a ❏
9c ❏	20a ❏	30a ❏	39b ❏	49b ❏
10a ❏	20b ❏	30b ❏	39c ❏	49c ❏
10b ❏	20c ❏		40a ❏	50a ❏
10c ❏			40b ❏	50b ❏
			40c ❏	50c ❏

Note your score below

Total = 150   Your score = ❏

So how did you do?

Scoring

Use the scoring grid below after you have completed the audit to work out how well you have done.

Every right answer receives 3 points.

Where there is definitely a single right answer the other options have no points linked to them. Where there is a hierarchy of responses and some are nearer to being 'right' than others, then choosing these other options means you will gain either one or two points.

1a	3	11a	1	21a	3			31a	1	41a	2
1b	1	11b	2	21b	0			31b	2	41b	3
1c	2	11c	3	22a	3			31c	3	41c	1
2a	1	12a	0	22b	1			32a	0	42a	1
2b	2	12b	0	22c	2			32b	0	42b	3
2c	3	12c	3	23a	0			32c	3	42c	2
3a	1	13a	3	23b	3			33a	3	43a	3
3b	3	13b	0	23c	0			33b	0	43b	0
3c	2	14a	3	24a	3			33c	0	43c	0
4a	0	14b	2	24b	0			34a	3	44a	2
4b	3	14c	1	25a	0			34b	0	44b	1
5a	1	15a	0	25b	3			35a	3	44c	3
5b	3	15b	3			26a	0	35b	0	45a	0
5c	2	16a	3			26b	3	35c	0	45b	3
6a	0	16b	0			26c	0	36a	3	46a	3
6b	3	17a	1			27a	1	36b	1	46b	1
7a	0	17b	3			27b	2	36c	2	46c	2
7b	0	17c	2			27c	3	37a	1	47a	1
7c	3	18a	1			28a	0	37b	2	47b	3
8a	3	18b	2			28b	0	37c	3	47c	2
8b	1	18c	3			28c	3	38a	3	48a	0
8c	2	19a	3			29a	0	38b	1	48b	0
9a	0	19b	2			29b	3	38c	2	48c	3
9b	0	19c	1			29c	0	39a	0	49a	2
9c	3	20a	3			30a	3	39b	3	49b	3
10a	1	20b	2			30b	0	39c	0	49c	1
10b	3	20c	1					40a	1	50a	3
10c	2							40b	1	50b	1
								40c	3	50c	2

Quick audit score: More than 55

Full audit score: More than 110

If you scored more than 110 points when completing the full audit or more than 55 when completing the quick audit, you are well on the way to addressing your personal work–life balance issues successfully and you may also be working in a school that supports your work–life balance aspirations. Striving to achieve the right work–life balance for you is already an integral part of your life. You understand the key work–life balance issues and you understand how they affect the different components of your life.

Quick audit score: 31–55

Full audit score: 66–110

If you scored between 66 and 110 points when completing the full audit or between 31 and 55 when completing the quick audit, you already have some awareness of the most important work–life balance issues. If you review your knowledge of the work–life balance agenda to see if you are keeping up to date with the issues, you will probably approach personal work–life balance planning with more confidence. Take time to work out how the major work–life balance issues impact upon your whole life and check very carefully to see if you are managing your time well.

You probably need to review your approach to how you manage the interface between your working life and your life outside work and to make sure that you understand how to create space to give you time to do the things you want to do.

Do a bit more research about work–life balance. Look at the list of useful websites at the end of this guide to help you to know where to start. Try to find time to update your personal work–life balance strategy.

Quick audit score: Up to 30

Full audit score: Up to 65

You need to start thinking seriously about work–life balance. You need to review your understanding of the work–life balance agenda and how it is being implemented in your school. You need to look carefully at your own approach to how you organise and manage your working life and your life outside work. You may also need to give more consideration to a range of related issues including your health and wellbeing, and your self-esteem and sense of self worth.

Do some research about work–life balance. Look at the list of useful websites at the end of this guide to help you to know where to start. Talk to people who you think are achieving sound work–life balance: then start working on your work–life balance strategy.

What next?

You will now have an indication of how well you are currently doing with work–life balance. If you completed the quick audit, you are ready to move on to Chapter 3.

If you completed the full audit you will find a more detailed analysis of your responses below.

About your score – full audit

There were 50 questions in the work–life balance audit. They deal with five major work–life balance development areas and there are ten questions linked to each of these areas.

1   Time management and personal effectiveness
2   Understanding the work–life balance agenda
3   Your school's approach to work–life balance
4   Self-esteem, self-worth and self-confidence
5   Your health and wellbeing

You will need to make sure you take all these issues into account if you are going to achieve sound work–life balance.

You will see that in the boxes below the question numbers have been arranged to indicate the key work–life balance theme that they reflect. Tick each of the questions in each of the five areas where you scored three points. Once you have done that you will see there are some areas where you did better than others when you completed the audit. You will also begin to see where your development areas could lie.

Review the guidance under each of the headings and bear this in mind as you work through the rest of the guide.

1 Time management and personal effectiveness

Question number	3	5	8	14	17	24	27	34	46	48
Did you score three points?										

If you didn't achieve three points for more than one of your answers to questions 3, 5, 8, 27 and 46 be careful about your willingness to respond to the demands people make of you. Your willingness to respond to the demands of others could be a factor in preventing you from achieving the work–life balance that is right for you. Chapter 3 deals with the issue of responsiveness in your working life. Chapter 4 deals with this issue in your life beyond work.

If you did not choose the right answers for questions 14, 24, 34 and 48 then you need to take a long hard look at how you manage your life. Chapter 4 looks in some depth at strategies to help you to create and use discretionary time to help you on your work–life balance journey.

If you did not get question 17 right, bear this in mind for when you come to review the notes on self-esteem, self-worth and self-confidence.

2 Understanding the work–life balance agenda

Question number	4	7	12	25	26	28	30	32	35	43
Did you score three points?										

The questions under this heading deal with work–life balance issues that are being addressed through legislation and through developments in the world of work. Some of the most common work–life balance issues faced by people, including teachers, are also raised here.

If you did not score particularly highly on this section you need to do some research about work–life balance generally. Being more knowledgeable about the work–life balance agenda will help you to know what types of issues are being dealt with via legislation and through other developments in the world of work. Use Chapter 5 in this guide and the bibliography to help you to broaden your understanding of work–life balance.

If you did not score three points for question 28, note that getting the right job description is one of the key stepping stones to achieving the work–life balance you want.

3   Your school's approach to work–life balance

Question number	1	2	10	16	20	31	36	38	40	41
Did you score three points?										

The questions in this section will help you to be more aware of how helpful the school where you work is in helping you to achieve the work–life balance which is right for you. Work–life balance is not about taking unilateral action yourself, nor is it something you can achieve on your own. Therefore you need to take the issues raised here into account when thinking about work–life balance and when choosing a school in which to work.

If your school doesn't have a work–life balance policy and does not ensure that work–life balance is on the management agenda, as indicated by your answers to questions 1, 3, 10 and 16, you need to consider the impact of this on your personal work–life balance and how you can ensure that work–life balance gains a higher profile in your school. Consider, too, how effectively your school supports work–life balance through reviewing your answers to questions 2, 31, 36, 38, 40 and 41.

4   Self-esteem, self-worth and self-confidence

Question number	11	15	18	19	22	37	39	42	44	47
Did you score three points?										

There's a lot of personal responsibility involved in achieving work–life balance. If you don't value yourself highly enough to prioritise your own plans above the needs, demands and expectations of others for at least some of the time, you'll never achieve the work–life balance you're looking for. You will always be servicing other people. Look again at questions 18, 19, 44 and 47 to see how you are doing with this issue.

You also need to consider the value you place on your own aspirations and if you actually allow yourself to succeed. Look at your responses to questions 15, 37 and 39 to help you here. Are you prepared to be clear about what you want and then to take action to get it? Review your answers to questions 11, 22 and 42 to see how you are doing.

If you have found that this is an area of development for you, then Chapter 4 in the guide is likely to be the most helpful to you. Review also your understanding of the difference between being busy and being effective and why you agree to complete tasks, both of which are dealt with in Chapter 3.

5   Your health and wellbeing

Question number	6	9	13	21	23	29	33	45	49	50
Did you score three points?										

Your health and wellbeing underpin your work–life balance, so you need to take care of them. You need to make sure you don't neglect these areas as you strive to succeed in all components of your life.

You need to be aware of the incidence and impact of work-related stress on your life, so review your scores for questions 21, 23, 33 and 49 to see if you have the right level of awareness. Remember, too, that having a life outside work is important, so consider how well you did with questions 6, 13, 45 and 50. Check out your understanding of health and wellbeing through your responses to questions 9 and 29.

Use Chapter 4 of the guide to help you with health and wellbeing issues. Chapter 3 looks at work-related stress and Chapter 5 notes where health and wellbeing programmes fit into the work–life balance agenda.

And finally . . .

If you would like staff in your school to sample the audit turn to Appendix 1.

Summary – key points

1   This section of the guide to work–life balance contains two work–life balance audits that will help you to establish where you are now on your work–life balance journey.

2   The quick audit comprises 25 questions on work–life balance issues.

3   The full audit comprises 50 multiple-choice questions built around five key work–life balance themes.

4   These themes are:
   ● Time management and personal effectiveness
   ● Understanding the work–life balance agenda
   ● Your school's approach to work–life balance
   ● Self-esteem, self-worth and self-confidence
   ● Your health and wellbeing.

5   When you complete the quick audit the guidance you receive will help you to gain an overview of your current approach to achieving work–life balance.

6   When you complete the full audit, as well as gaining that overview, you can review your scores and responses to particular questions in depth to help you to establish where your particular strengths and development areas are with reference to work–life balance.

7 Use the results of the audit to guide your reading and research on work–life balance issues and to help you as you work through this guide.

CHAPTER 3

Work–life balance and work

Overview

Taking control of your working life is the first stage on your work–life balance journey and this task is the focus of Chapter 3 of this guide. As you work through this chapter you will analyse your job, your working environment, the support you receive from your school with work–life balance and your own part in this important task. By completing the activities at the end of this section you will begin to lay the foundations for your future work–life balance.

Introduction

Most teachers begin to think about work–life balance in the context of their work. This makes a lot of sense. Poor work–life balance is often primarily the result of the work element of your life getting out of control. When work takes over your life other activities get squeezed out and, as a result, your work–life balance suffers.

Most people with poor work–life balance believe they are to blame for their situation. They spend a lot of time and energy striving to reach impossible goals and then criticising themselves for their shortcomings when they fail to reach them.

It's true that you have the overall responsibility for managing your working life and for achieving sound work–life balance, but the culture of your school and the ways in which work is organised and managed in your school also play a big part in the work–life balance equation. Therefore, if you are looking to improve your work–life balance you need to think about:

- the influence the culture of your school has on your work–life balance
- how the working environment affects your work–life balance
- your own part in managing your working life to help to achieve sound work–life balance.

Your school's culture

Choosing the right school

It's probably not the most helpful suggestion for anyone working in a school that does not help its staff to achieve sound work–life balance to begin this section by talking about job hunting. However, putting work–life balance issues on the agenda when you are thinking about taking up a post in a school is really important.

When you are looking for a job, and investigate a school where you think you might like to work, remember to check about the school's approach to work–life balance issues. Think about at least some of the following questions:

1 Do people on the staff have an understanding of what work–life balance is?

2 Does this school have a work–life balance policy?

3 Do staff in school give the impression that they have achieved the right work–life balance for them?

4 Is work–life balance on the management agenda? (Is work–life balance an important issue in the school?)

5 Is work–life balance for every one, not just for teachers?

6 Are governors involved in helping people – including the head teacher – to achieve sound work–life balance?

7 Does the school's approach to health and safety issues encompass activities to ensure that staff do not suffer from work-related stress?

8 Do senior staff in school accept that people have a right to a life outside work?

9 How does the head teacher respond when you ask about work–life balance?

10 Do you think the head has got things right in this school as far as work–life balance is concerned?

You might also ask the same questions about your current school in order to assess just how much support you currently get to help you to achieve sound work–life balance.

The working environment

What about your current job?

However, choosing your next school is a task for the future. In the real world and in the here and now, you need to go right back to the basic nuts and bolts of the job you have at present and ask: Is my job do-able?

This is a question which most teachers do not ask. They ask instead: Can I do this job? This is the wrong starting point. That question throws responsibility back onto teachers themselves and can lead to their thinking they have major shortcomings when, in fact, the job they are trying to do may be an impossible one.

So, focus first on the job itself. There's no point in your thinking of ever more sophisticated ways of managing your workload or asking for more training in the content of the job, if the job is too large for one person or if you lack the support you need to enable you to complete the tasks your job demands of you.

Even with the advent of workforce remodelling and reviews of teaching and learning responsibilities, there is a strong possibility that some roles in school just cannot be done by one person, whether the role holder spends 35, 40, 60 or 90 hours a week at work.

So remember, keep the focus first on the requirements of the job, not on you and your abilities.

Review your job description and think about how your job was designed in the first place. Often the problem is that the job was never really designed. Many jobs in schools were established a long time ago and have had bits added to them as new tasks have emerged. Also, in the case of many jobs, whether they are associated with delivering the curriculum, the management of the curriculum or the management of the school, they will almost certainly have been designed by senior managers thinking about all the things which need to be done and then dividing those tasks up among the number of people available to do them.

Even today, there are lots of jobs in school where the questions about:

- the purpose of the job
- the level and scope of responsibility that comes with the job
- the workload associated with the job
- the physical and mental demands of the job
- the skills people need to do the job

have just not been considered in sufficient depth when a set of responsibilities is parcelled up and handed to someone as a job.

Job descriptions, too, are often imprecise and can simply comprise a list of tasks which inevitably includes a catch-all phrase about other duties as reasonably requested by the head teacher, so teachers tend to think they have no choice but to do – or to try to do – all that is asked of them.

Activity 3.1, at the end of the chapter, deals with your job and asks you to analyse whether it really is do-able. Completing the activity will help you to establish what steps you need to take to make sure you have a job which can be done.

Complete the activity now if you would like to reflect on your job immediately. Complete it when you have finished reading the chapter if you would prefer to do all the activities together.

Now that you have begun to do some serious thinking about your own job, look around you. Are other people in school having difficulty in fulfilling their responsibilities? If they are then the issue of job viability affects more people in school than you. In this situation you will need to start to ask questions about job redesign, job evaluation and the review of job descriptions, not just for yourself but for others too. Remember that the task will be much easier if you can get other people's support and present a proposal to senior management from a whole group rather than from yourself alone.

However, if you find that other people are coping with their jobs you need to do two things:

- review your own skills and expertise, especially if you have only recently taken on your current role, and be prepared to ask for more training
- look for additional support in school to help you to do your job.

When you think about your expertise and your ability to do the job ask if there is a person specification linked to your job. Have a look at it to see what skills, experience, qualifications etc. have been defined as necessary for this role. If you do not have that expertise, then, as a matter of urgency, you need to set about gaining it.

If there is no person specification think about writing a draft and asking one of the school's senior team to help you establish just what expertise a person needs in order to do your job.

Alternatively, or in addition to the above, you might need some additional support from people already doing the job, or from those who know the details of the job, to help you reach the required level, especially if you have just taken on the role.

Go on that course, or shadow a more experienced person. Ask questions about your job. If you know in specific terms what you want to learn more about, your school is more likely to find ways to help you to undertake development activities.

Long hours: the twenty-first-century bane

The long hours culture is a huge problem in workplaces throughout the western world. With more than 17 per cent of the population in the United Kingdom working more than forty-eight hours a week, and increasing numbers of people, especially those in professional and managerial roles, working more than sixty hours a week, it is a problem which is getting worse, so the chances are that in order to preserve or to achieve sound work–life balance you will have to learn how to deal with the long hours ethos in a school where you are working at some point in your career.

On the surface it looks great that people are willing to work extra hours for no more pay. Why should any employer protest about voluntary unpaid overtime undertaken by a willing workforce?

ALMOST TIME FOR SOME ME TIME

If, for the sake of your work–life balance, you wish to challenge the culture of working excessive numbers of hours, above all you need to distance your challenge from your personal circumstances and challenge the long hours culture on the grounds of:

● health and safety
● productivity – your school's performance and the performance of individual teachers.

Working long hours is bad for productivity and bad for you as a teacher. People work less efficiently when they work longer and longer hours. They are more likely to make mistakes. They have more accidents and their health suffers. Their rates of work slow down and they often work less effectively over a longer period at work than they did when they worked shorter hours and took more breaks. This really is a situation where more can often mean less. What's more, those who analyse working practices have been saying this for almost a hundred years.

So think about the hours you work and ask the following questions:

- Does your school actually value your time?
- Are you helped to work efficiently?

In short:

- Does your school help you to use your time wisely?

If your school does not value your time at least some of your efforts will be wasted. So think carefully:

- Are you given a clear indication of what is expected of you?
- Are you helped to prioritise your work, to know what you need to do first?
- Does your school make sure there is no unnecessary duplication of effort?
- Does your school make sure there is no wasted effort?

Thinking a little more broadly:

- Does your school resource teachers adequately in terms of computers, teaching materials, availability of support staff etc.?
- Does your school train teachers and other staff to be able to use the computer software and time-saving equipment in classrooms or subject areas?
- Does your school take tasks away from teachers that could be done by other people?
- Are the senior people in your school careful not to give staff too much to do all at once?

And do you play your part in using time wisely? If your school is trying to help you to make better use of your time do you co-operate with those efforts? Do you make sure you can use all the equipment and other resources available to you? Do you hand over those tasks which can be done by those who are not teachers – even the tasks you like doing – to support staff, for example to teaching assistants? Do you try to find the most time-efficient ways of completing jobs?

These are important questions because one of the biggest problems with the long hours culture is that people who work long hours often see working even more hours as the only solution to every problem they encounter. They lose the ability to judge when to stop working, when to ask for help with their work and when to refuse a task because it is outside their remit or because they are already overloaded. Teachers in this situation need help from senior staff to see their work from a different perspective and to accept that there are limits to what they can do and what can legitimately be expected of them.

If you find you are working longer and longer and there is no-one to encourage you to stop, then try to step back from your work just long enough to reflect on this section of the guide or force yourself to discuss your approach to your work with a colleague or friend. Ask yourself: Is there another way of approaching my work?

Rest assured that there are other ways. Keep looking until you find one of them and read the rest of this chapter to help you to find the answers.

All present and correct: a bad thing for your school

Sometimes the long hours culture in a school manifests itself in the guise of 'presenteeism'. Presenteeism thrives in organisations where people's worth is judged by the number of hours they spend on school premises rather than by their achievements and where there is pressure from other staff or from managers to be seen to be at work.

Being present and available and, yes, visible, are perceived as good things in these schools. Presenteeism is endorsed where people who are always at school are the ones who are rewarded with promotions, and thus they set expectations of time to be spent at work for the next tier of managers or teachers. As a result, every one tries to arrive in school before other staff and to stay in school at least as long as other people in the evening. In some schools, for example, no-one goes home before the head teacher because they think they should be seen to be at work. This can lead to people being in work for 12 hours a day and feeling guilty if they go home at a reasonable time or while other people are still in school.

Look at the number of hours you spend in school and consider the following:

- Do you decide on the amount of time you spend in school with reference to the expectations of others and the amount of time other people spend in school?
- Do you stay in school late or arrive early because everyone else does?
- If you focused on the needs of the job rather than the expectations and behaviours of others, would your attendance patterns change?

Ask the question:

- Isn't it more important to look at what people achieve than to judge their success by the length of time they spend in school?

Remember that valuing and rewarding what people are seen to be doing rather than what they achieve is poor management practice.

If you are a victim of the culture of presenteeism then you need to speak up about the importance of your school rewarding achievement rather than visibility.

Make the point that people should be appraised and judged on the basis of the targets they have met and the standards they and their learners have achieved, not on the number of hours they have spent at work. If you have managerial responsibilities yourself, apply those same principles when dealing with your staff members: reward achievement, not time-serving.

Stress: isn't that for wimps?

Work-related stress is a problem for many teachers and it is high on the list of factors contributing to poor work–life balance for people in schools and elsewhere. More than half of all teachers diagnose themselves as suffering from stress that has been at least in part induced by their jobs. When people suffer from this type of stress it can affect their whole lives so it is important to treat it seriously.

Many teachers think that to be suffering from work-related stress is to fail in some way. They are often reluctant to say that their work is stressful because they think they will be judged inadequate. Even if they say nothing about the stress they are suffering, they often make this judgement about themselves and, as a result, suffer low self-esteem too. Stress is also a problem because some people say they thrive on stress and that stress is for wimps. Hence, by implication anyone who suffers from stress is a wimp. Also teachers who suffer from stress have often been told that teaching is a stressful job so they should expect to be stressed.

Yet there is also a lot of misunderstanding about stress. Some stress is indeed helpful. It can motivate and help you to achieve, but unhealthy stress results when there is a mismatch between what you can do in your job and what is expected of you. This type of stress can undermine everything you do, demotivate you and destroy your pleasure in your work. It can also cause serious ill health. This is the type of stress which you should try to avoid.

Stress is defined by the Health and Safety Executive (HSE) as: 'the adverse reaction people have to excessive pressure or other types of demand placed on them'. When you begin to think about dealing with stress, and especially work-related stress, focus, first, not on yourself but on employers' obligations to help their employees to avoid work-related stress and to help them deal with stressful situations when they occur. Ask the question: Is your school helping teachers to avoid work-related stress?

For example, employers have a responsibility to undertake risk assessments of the working environment and to take steps to reduce health hazards, including work-related stress. The outcome of these risk assessments could require your school to reorganise work or to reshape jobs to help to make them less stressful in the terms defined above.

As far as you are aware has your school undertaken this type of risk assessment? Take the time to find out and ask for one to be completed – not for yourself but for the benefit of everyone.

Encourage your school to approach work-related stress in terms of:

- the demands of the job
- the type of support you need to enable you to do the job
- the ways in which your school can help you to have a less stressful working life.

Activity 3.2, at the end of the chapter, deals with the culture of your school and considers whether or not your school's approach to some of the issues raised above is helpful to someone looking to establish sound work–life balance.

Complete the activity now if you would like to focus on your school's input into your work–life balance immediately. Complete it when you have finished reading the chapter if you would prefer to do all the activities together.

Your own part in managing your working life

Getting back on track

If your work has begun to take over your whole life, getting back on track and re-establishing sound work–life balance will require careful planning on your part and on the production and implementation of a clear remedial strategy.

Remember that getting back on track is not about taking unilateral action, talking loudly about your rights and stating what you will and will not be doing in the future. The main reason to avoid the unilateral action is that it sets you apart from everyone else in school. This is a mistake. So many aspects of achieving and then sustaining sound work–life balance are about looking at your school's culture and working environment and seeing how they can be shaped to help everyone including yourself. Unilateral action prevents you from working collaboratively with your school to try to improve the work–life balance of everyone.

You won't be surprised to hear that many people have tried the unilateral approach and found it doesn't work. They may be pressured in carrying on much the same as before or they may be viewed as eccentrics or difficult people. Once they have been labelled in this way they are often also labelled as people who do not really care about school and therefore are not people who are suitable for promotion. Little wonder then that some people believe you are committing career suicide if you set out on the work–life balance journey.

However, you know you want to improve your work–life balance, so you also need to understand just how important it is to take control of your working life. To begin with, you need to work through some or all of the above issues. It is very important to review:

- your job
- your working environment

but you also need to remember that you have a part to play in achieving the work–life balance you want.

Remember that if you want to find a major cause of your own poor work–life balance, you probably need to do no more than to stand in front of a mirror and point at the person you see.

Time is a finite resource

When you begin to think about your own part in achieving the work–life balance you want, think first about the ways in which you allocate and use your time.

There are some very simple truths about time which people often forget. Time is very neatly parcelled up into clearly defined units. There are

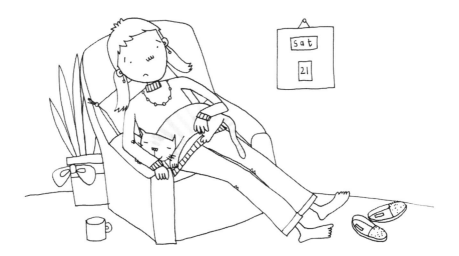

TOO TIRED TO EAT, TOO TIRED TO DO THE GARDEN. YIPEE! IT'S THE WEEKEND!

24 hours in a day, 168 hours in a week, 52 weeks in a year, and no-one has any more or less time than anyone else.

If you find yourself saying the following:

- If only there were more hours in the day
- I'll do the job myself – it's quicker
- Everything I do always takes longer than I planned
- Time flies – I don't know where the morning/afternoon/day has gone
- I can't ask someone else to do this job – no-one else can do it right
- I don't have time to sit down and explain that task/procedure
- I could cope, but only if there weren't so many interruptions

you need to review the ways in which you use your time. For example: are you sure you use your working time wisely?

Work often spills over into the various components of people's lives because they forget the basic rule about time: **time is a finite resource**. This could mean that you also forget that if you take extra time to complete something in one part of your life, you have less time to spend in another.

If you're happy with the ways in which you distribute and use your time there is no problem. If you have allowed school to take up more of your time than you think is right, you need to consider very carefully how you allocate your time.

Allocating your time – what shall I do first?

When you have a lot to do you need to think carefully about how you prioritise your efforts. You need to ensure that you allocate most of your available time to tasks in three categories:

- the tasks that only you can do – those which use your special skills
- the tasks that are really important to your job – the key results areas of your job by which your success will be judged

- the real crises and emergencies which schools have to deal with from time to time – if you think there are crises and emergencies every day then readjust your definition of a crisis or an emergency.

When you are next asked to take on a task, knowing that time is a finite resource, ask yourself:

- Does this job/task need to be done at all?
- Does this job/task need to be done now?
- Does it need to be done by me? (Is this part of my responsibility?)
- Am I the best person to do this job/task?
- Will I be encroaching on someone else's job/responsibility if I take on this job/task?
- If I take on this job/task what will I not be able to do with the time I use on it?
- If I take on this job/task will I be unable to do something that is really important in my role?

When you have asked yourself these questions note if taking the time to think about these issues results in your behaving differently.

Opportunity knocks

Most schools try to encourage collaborative working. Teamworking, sharing tasks and responsibilities and working together on action plans are all good for morale. Most teachers value the opportunity to help other people, especially their colleagues. Teachers are often keen to tell people that one of the reasons they came into teaching was to help others.

Thus, when someone – a colleague or a senior person in school – asks you to do something, the chances are you will respond positively; you will give your time. You will be willing to spend extra time with parents or with learners, and all of this is beneficial to you and to your school – up to a point.

However, you need to be aware that when you are doing one task you lose the opportunity to complete another. You cannot conduct an interview

I'VE FOUND A NEW WAY TO STOP BEING
SO RESPONSIVE

You might be efficient in what you do but are you also effective?

Ask yourself, are you climbing the right mountain, or are you too busy to ask yourself that sort of question?

The responsive teacher

In many schools, if teachers do not take on additional tasks simply because they can do the job, they take them on because someone has asked them to do so.

Responding to needs, being helpful, working collaboratively and, of course, responding swiftly and professionally to emergencies, are all excellent behaviours, but if they are demonstrated in excess they damage your work–life balance and your ability to do your job.

It can be very difficult to refuse requests for help and support, but, once again, you need to remember that by responding to everyone's requests you will be unable to do your own work and there is a good chance that your work–life balance will suffer.

- Learning to say 'no' is a necessary part of fulfilling your responsibilities in school

- Learning to say 'no' is a necessary part of achieving and sustaining the right work–life balance for you

Remember also that people will willingly use your time to save theirs. People approach those they know will listen to them and help them, and they probably know how difficult you find it to turn them away. When they come into your classroom or interrupt your marking they are taking over your working life. If this happens to you a lot, then ask:

- Are you waiting to be interrupted?
- Do you want someone to prevent you from doing this boring/difficult task?
- Do you encourage people to interrupt you?

Try also to think about the impact of your responsiveness on the people you are helping. Ask yourself:

- Is being responsive really helping people or not?

You may be providing help, but as a teacher you know the best support you can give is to help someone to be able to do a task without your help. By being so responsive are you sometimes preventing people from extending their abilities? Do you take this into account when you decide to respond to a request? On some occasions might it be the best solution not to be available to help or to help someone with only part of a task?

Does no really mean yes?

For some teachers the real problem is not in identifying the issues they need to deal with but in taking action to change the way they deal with requests to be responsive. In particular, many teachers have real difficulty in saying 'no' and meaning it.

Is this your problem? When someone asks you for help and you really want to refuse the request, do you begin by saying 'no', hesitate, move to 'maybe', then, before you know where you are, agree to do something you know you neither have the time to do nor really want to?

Some of the most common situations in which teachers struggle to say no follow. When you are next faced with any of them try the solutions offered.

Example 1

Someone wants your advice and says: 'It'll only take a minute'.

Are you really still falling for that one? If the issue will take a minute to resolve you can probably spare that minute. You should offer a minute and only a minute. If the issue is going to take longer to deal with – and in most cases it will – ask the person to schedule time to come back and talk to you later in the day. As often as not, people find they can deal with their issue without you if you don't respond immediately.

Example 2

A senior person in school asks you to take on an additional task when you are already overloaded. When this happens you need to make that person aware of your situation politely and professionally. Do you explain that by doing this new task another task will have to be displaced? Do you explain that other deadlines may have to shift? Do you make it clear that there is a consequence to your agreeing to the new task? In the end, do you ask for clarification on which task you should do first?

Example 3

Whenever people ask you to help them you agree because you worry about what people will think of you if you refuse.

If this is the case then you need to be more aware of your reasons for agreeing to take on the task and review them. Will people really like you less if you sometimes say no?

Also ask yourself, does it matter if they do? If that is the way they make their decisions about people, do you really value their judgements?

You know from experience just how your inability to say no gets in the way of some of the things you want to do with your life. You know that to help you to take control of your life you must build a repertoire of responses which will help you to say no when you want to say no and stick to your decision.

Start with the strategies noted to help you deal with the situations above and build on them.

Making the most of your working time

Much of the guidance in this section has been about saving time and using time wisely, but remember that you have been making time for a purpose. This is an area which is explored in Chapter 4.

However, before leaving this chapter, note that if you need further help with the issues raised here, there is a whole industry surrounding time management, making time and getting more out of time. You may find it useful to look at some of this guidance, provided you remember that the most important way of establishing control over your working life is to use time wisely.

Now that you have finished reading this chapter, complete activity 3.3 and any of the other activities linked to this chapter you have not yet considered.

Summary – key points

1 In order to take control of your working life you need to think about the culture of your school, your working environment and your own part in managing your working life.
2 Try to choose to work in a school where they take work–life balance seriously.
3 Wherever you are working, review your job description and how your job has been designed to ensure that it is both manageable and it reflects what you should be doing.
4 Take steps to ensure that this is the job you do.
5 Remember that time is a finite resource and that every choice you make about how to use your time has opportunity costs linked to it.
6 Ask yourself if your school values your time and helps you to use it wisely.

7 Review your own approach both to deciding on how many hours to work and how much time to spend on school premises carefully because the long-hours culture is a huge problem in workplaces today. Working excessive hours can damage productivity and create health and safety problems for individuals and for schools.

8 Review whether your school is helping people to avoid work-related stress and if, on balance, you think it is a good place to work.

9 When you come to review your own role in controlling your working life, avoid unilateral action as this isolates you from the rest of the staff.

10 Focus on the tasks which only you can do, on those which are really important to your job and on real crises and emergencies.

11 Be prepared to say no to inappropriate requests for your assistance and to question whether some tasks need to be done at all, or whether you are the right person to do them.

12 Beware of accepting tasks just because you can do them or simply because someone has asked you to do them.

13 Remember it is more important to do the right thing than to do lots of things and that there is a significant difference between being busy and being effective.

14 Above all, learn to make the most of your working time.

Activities

These activities will help you to take control of your working life. All three activities are also suitable for school-based staff development sessions.

Activity 3.1 can also be used to support the appraisal and performance management process.

ACTIVITY 3.1: CAN ANYONE DO MY JOB?

Use this activity to help you to establish if your job can be done.

Can anyone do my job?

Look at your current job description.

Does your job have a relevant title?

Does your job description note to whom you report and where you fit into the school's structure?

Does your job description state the grade or salary range of the job (not the actual salary)? (Optional element.)

Is the main **purpose** of your job clearly stated? (Is there a statement which answers the question: Why does this job exist?)

If there is a **job purpose** statement, does it accurately reflect the requirements of your job today? If it does not, then summarise the purpose of your current job in a single statement, e.g. *Under the direction of the head of humanities to teach history and geography to learners in years 7 to 11*. If you cannot summarise your job succinctly, review your role with your head teacher or with another senior person in school.

Are the **key results areas** or **required outcomes** or **success criteria** for the job stated? (Is there an indication of what you need to achieve in your job?), e.g. *To ensure that the learners for whom the role holder is responsible are taught history and geography in accordance with the relevant school-based schemes of work (years 7 to 9) and in accordance with relevant examining body requirements (years 10 to 11).*

Are the **main activities** or **tasks** of your job stated accurately? (Is there a list of what is expected of you or what you need to do to fulfil the purpose of the job?), e.g. *to conduct termly assessments of learners' progress using the published departmental assessment criteria.*

Is the relevant **job knowledge** stated? (Are the knowledge levels and other requirements someone will need to do the job stated? Are the school-based job knowledge requirements stated?), e.g. *awareness and understanding of current schemes of work and examining body requirements; up-to-date knowledge of developments in the teaching of history and geography.*

Is there a **catch-all** statement about doing other duties as required by the governors/head teacher/head of department? If there is, work out how much of your time you spend on these other duties. If it is more than 10 per cent of your time, ask about having your job redefined.

If your job is already defined accurately, check if this is the job you are currently doing. If this is not the job you are doing, ask yourself is it the job you should be doing? If it is, take action to realign your activities with the job. If it isn't, you need a new job description and you need to speak to your head teacher or other senior person in school about getting one.

If, having adjusted your work to fit the job description, you find you cannot do the job, establish why. It could be because of the *size* of the job, or that you do not have the *skills* you need to do the job, or the level of *support* you need to achieve the required results is not available. Once you are clear why your job cannot be done, you will need to speak to your head teacher or other senior person in school about strategies for making the job viable.

If your current job is not reflected accurately in your job description, and if you think you are currently doing the job you should be doing, produce a statement which more accurately reflects your job. Use the emboldened terms in this activity (purpose, key results areas etc.) to help you.

Try to work out how many hours a week it will take to complete the requirements of this job. If, when you have done this, you find the job is not do-able, think about what could be removed from the job to make it more manageable.

You then need to speak to the head teacher or other senior person in school about reviewing your job more formally.

ACTIVITY 3.2: YOUR WHOLE-SCHOOL CULTURE AND WORK–LIFE BALANCE

Use this activity to help you to establish if the culture of your school is supportive of teachers' work–life balance aspirations.

Your whole-school culture and work–life balance

The questions below draw attention to some of the main ways in which all schools can help their staff to improve their work–life balance. The key issues are emboldened.

Give your school a rating on a scale of 1 to 10, with 1 indicating a negative response and 10 indicating a wholly positive response.

1 Does your school have a **work–life balance policy**?

2 Does your school take the issue of **work-related stress** seriously?

3 Does everyone in school have **clearly defined responsibilities?**

4 Are managers in school tackling the **long-hours culture?**

5 Does your school actively seek to remove the causes of **work-related stress?**

Q1	1	2	3	4	5	6	7	8	9	10
Q2	1	2	3	4	5	6	7	8	9	10
Q3	1	2	3	4	5	6	7	8	9	10
Q4	1	2	3	4	5	6	7	8	9	10
Q5	1	2	3	4	5	6	7	8	9	10

Where you have indicated a response between 1 and 6, note what you think the impact of your school's approach is on your personal work–life balance, e.g. *Our school does not have a work–life balance policy, so people just don't take work–life balance issues into account when they are handing out tasks. This means I am regularly overloaded and have to take a lot of my work home. I have to do school work for several hours each weekend when I would rather be doing other things.*

What can you yourself do to improve the situation with reference to each of the questions where you have noted your responses are in the shaded sections?

What work–life balance issues need to be taken up with your senior staff?

Consider how you might demonstrate to your senior team that taking action on these work–life balance issues will help:

● individual teachers

● your whole school.

This activity looks at Sam, a year 6 class teacher in a large primary school. It deals with how Sam deals with a typical lunch time in school.

Put yourself in Sam's shoes and at the end of each paragraph decide what you would do next. Try not to read ahead as you work through the activity.

Be honest about your responses, because we probably all know what we should do, even Sam! The problem is that in the moment we often behave very differently from what would be the best course of action for ourselves and for our work–life balance.

1 It is coming up to one o'clock and you are on your way to the staff room for lunch. The telephone rings as you enter the staff room. You are nearest the phone and you pick it up. It is the mother of a child in your class. It soon becomes clear that she wishes to speak to you at length about her son. What do you do in Sam's situation?

2 It's just after one o'clock and you're on the telephone to a parent. The temp from the school office signals to you that you have another call. Her scribbled note says that it's the inspector from the local police station with whom you have been negotiating for over a month about his participation in a school social event. He wants to discuss possible dates and his involvement in the event with his superior officer at 1.30 p.m. He has a query about the message you left for him last night. What do you do in Sam's situation?

3 You have just spent ten minutes on the telephone to the police inspector and have made yourself a note to remind you to ring the parent after school. You didn't pass on your annoyance, but you think the message you had originally left had been quite clear. While on the phone you have been rummaging in your briefcase and carrier bags for your lunch and, as a result, forgot to summarise what you had agreed with the inspector at the end of the call. You hesitate with the telephone receiver still in your hand about what to do next because you are uncertain about his understanding of the options for his involvement in the event. What do you do in Sam's situation?

4 As you begin to dial the inspector's number the newly-qualified teacher (NQT) in your key stage interrupts you and asks about some resources you said you were going to buy to help with the teaching of science. You break off from dialling to deal with the NQT. You remember that you haven't sent the order as yet and rush to your own classroom to find something that she can use until you have time to place the order. You can't find the resources you want immediately and you begin to feel anxious because you know the NQT is relying on you. What do you do in Sam's situation?

5   After finding some alternative, but not entirely suitable, resources you race back to the staff room. You apologise to the NQT because you don't have time to go through these resources with her. You then find that you haven't got your sandwiches after all. They must be at home on the kitchen table. You are beginning to feel a little bit light-headed because you didn't have breakfast and were on duty at morning break when tea and biscuits were available in the staff room. You know the coffee shop down the road will probably still have some sandwiches left. You check the time and decide that, although it will be a rush, you might still be able to get something to eat and get back in time for the start of the afternoon session, provided there isn't a queue in the shop. What do you do in Sam's situation?

6   As you head for the staff room door, on your way to the coffee shop, you see a note in your pigeon-hole. It is from the deputy head. It says that the 2.30 p.m. group singing activity has been pushed back to 3.00 p.m. and that the deputy head would like to see your class at the beginning of the afternoon. You try to find the deputy head to explain that you might be a few minutes late back from lunch but you can't find her. You scribble her a note but decide not to leave it. Your lunch break is almost over. What do you do in Sam's situation?

7   It is 2.10 p.m. Your heart is pounding and you are breathless in the school entrance hall, having raced back from the coffee shop. As you pause for breath at the foot of the stairs, sandwich and sandwich wrapping in hand, the head calls your name. He asks if you are all right as he has just been with your unattended class.

8   You will find something to say to your head teacher and later you will find that you misread the note from the deputy, but . . .

    . . . Are you having a successful day?

If you were acting as a mentor to Sam, and were using the guidance in Chapter 3 to help you to guide this teacher, what would you say to Sam about:

● using time wisely

● being responsive to others

● being clear about priorities

● being busy rather than effective

● work-related stress

● taking time to meet one's own needs?

Which parts of the advice you have offered Sam do you think you should heed in your own working life?

Possible answers

Whatever else you choose to discuss with Sam you need to ask the question: Who is in charge of Sam's life?

Sam is trying to do too much and without any real sense of where priorities lie. He/she is responding to just about everyone. He/she wants to help people and wants to be supportive. In behaving like this, Sam is neglecting personal needs. Missing meals is clearly having an impact. Light-headedness from lack of food is a bad sign. The levels of stress from which Sam suffers in trying to fit so much into the lunch break are not promoting his/her wellbeing.

The job that is Sam's responsibility is managing the police inspector's relationship with the school. Sam is not giving this task sufficient attention.

You might also review the concept of being busy rather than effective with Sam in the context of the interaction with the NQT.

CHAPTER 4

Life beyond work

Overview

This section of the guide takes you beyond looking at ways to take control of your working life to consider how you manage your life outside work. It will help you to take control of these other areas of your life just as you are now able to control your working life.

This chapter will also help you to be clear on what you want out of life, to define the work–life balance you are looking for and to decide where you wish to set the boundaries between your working life and your life outside work.

Getting control of your life outside work

Congratulations on having reached this section of the guide to work–life balance for teachers.

Making sure you have a manageable job is an essential part of the work–life balance equation, but there is still more you need to do before you arrive at your work–life balance goal. To get there you will need to review how you manage your life outside work and to take action to deal with the issues in that part of your life which are preventing you from achieving sound work–life balance.

If you are to achieve the work–life balance you are looking for, you need to take control of this area of your life just as you have done with your working life. If you don't, then it is likely that as your working life becomes manageable your life outside work will overwhelm you.

Taking control of your life outside work will almost certainly be more difficult than taking control of your life in school because there is a very broad range of activities, tasks and responsibilities vying for your attention and for your time outside work, and you do not have the structure of a job description or the direction of a line manager to help you to decide what to do.

Also, many of the situations you deal with outside work are more complex than those you find in school. Relationships can be more charged, situations more complex and making a success of activities outside work can be more important to you than anything you ever attempt at work. Indeed, so complex are the issues to be dealt with outside work that some people choose to spend more time at work and work longer and longer hours to avoid having to deal with them.

Discretion is everything

Your key objective now is to create more discretionary time, time which is yours to allocate as you see fit. You create discretionary time by using all your time, not just your working time, wisely.

Discretionary time is the raw material from which you will create your work–life balance successes. You use discretionary time to think, to plan and to reflect on what is important and to fulfil your aspirations. Once you have created discretionary time you will be able to focus on the task of working out exactly what you want in all aspects of your life. Only then will you be able to set the boundaries between your working life and your life outside work in the right place for you, and achieve the work–life balance that you have been looking for.

You have been creating discretionary time through the actions you have taken as a result of working through Chapter 3. Before leaving that chapter behind:

- confirm that you really have managed to take control of your working life and contained your work within what you think are reasonable limits
- decide which of the lessons you learned in Chapter 3 you need to apply to your life outside work.

Containing work

By now you will have taken some significant steps towards taking control of your working life and understanding how and why working life can take over the rest of your life.

However, you have not quite finished thinking about your working life. Before you turn your attention elsewhere review just how much of your time outside work you allocate to work-related tasks and make sure you have contained your work within what you consider to be reasonable limits.

For most teachers it is unrealistic to suggest that they do not bring work home, but you should make a judgement about how much of your life outside work you want to allocate to school work and how much you enjoy the work you do at home. The less you enjoy what you are doing with your time and the more resentful you feel about working at home, the more swiftly you need to act to contain work activities.

Whatever your feelings about your work, make sure you set aside time for things other than work.

There will always be enough work to fill whatever time you have so you will need to take action to reclaim your evenings, weekends and holidays if you have allowed work to take over your life. You need to make certain that your home has not – or does not – just become an extension of your workplace.

To help you to achieve your goals keep your school work in one part of your home. Don't allow those books which you haven't marked yet to glare at you when you are trying to watch television, eat a meal or play with your children. Keep them away from the parts of your home where you relax. Switch off from school for part of every evening and aim to keep most of each weekend for things other than work. If you bring marking home or prepare your teaching at home, don't let it swamp your evenings and weekends. Allow an amount of time during the weekend for these tasks. When that time has been used up, do something else.

Be disciplined. If you must check your e-mails over the weekend then maybe you need separate e-mail accounts for work and for your life

NO, SHE'S NOT DRUNK, SHE'S JUST A TEACHER

outside work. And, of course, try not to respond to e-mails related to school except at the times you have set aside to do school work.

Same problem – same solution

When thinking about your life outside work consider: Do you experience the same problems outside work as you encounter in school?

You may find, just as you did in school, that you have too much to do and not enough time in which to do it outside work. It could be that family and loved ones expect you to respond and be available to deal with their issues at any time, just as people at school expect you to be immediately responsive. It may be that your children, or your partner, or friends who have become accustomed to accessing your help on their terms – that is when they want it – need to learn that you cannot respond to them and do things for them all the time.

The bad news is that if you have the same problems in your life outside work as you experience in school there is something about your approach to your life which helps to create them. The good news is that you have already shown you can deal with these problems in your working life so there is no reason why you should not do the same in your life outside work too.

You already know where to start. Review the key learning points from the last section. The most important of these are:

- Time is a finite resource
- There are opportunity costs associated with every decision you make about how you use your time
- Learning to say no is a necessary part of achieving and sustaining the right work–life balance for you
- You need to understand the difference between being busy and effective
- You need to take care that you do not take on tasks and responsibilities on the basis of your ability to complete them, without reference to the time you have available.

From today, start to apply the same principles for taking control of your life outside work that you applied when you were reviewing your approach to your work.

The responsive person

Thinking about your responsiveness is a good place to begin to review your approach to your life beyond work. As a teacher you are responsive to the needs of others at work. You are probably also responsive to people in your life outside work. It is in your nature. One of your strengths is your ability to empathise with people and their problems. Your problem is that you respond to a great many needs, more, in fact, than you can cope with. This can get in the way of your work–life balance aspirations.

You need to think about the consequences of responding to so many different people and in so many different circumstances because, just as time is a finite resource, so too is your personal resource, and hence your ability to respond.

You could drain and exhaust yourself in the short term or burn yourself out in the medium term if you try to respond to everyone. You could also find that you struggle and sometimes fail to rise to the challenge of the real emergencies we all face in our lives.

Think about your responsiveness in terms of your bank account. Each act of responsiveness takes money out of your account. There will come a point with your bank account and with your ability to respond when you have no more resource; when, in fact, you will be unable to respond whether you would wish to or not.

Just as your savings and your ability to borrow money are both finite so is your personal resource. It is important not to use up all your savings or your borrowing capacity heedlessly.

You will know why this is important if you have ever expended a lot of energy at school and come home exhausted and emotionally drained only to find that you also need to offer extensive support in your family or in a relationship that really matters to you. If you have faced this situation, you will know what it feels like to be too worn out to help the people who matter to you as well as you would like.

By responding indiscriminately you leave yourself no margin to ensure you will be able to respond to crisis situations and to people who really matter to you when they need you.

Think now about prioritising your responsiveness with reference to what is really important to you, not simply with reference to the needs, demands and expectations of all the people you encounter.

Are you going to succeed with this?

Some people say that success is less about actions than it is about belief. If you believe you are going to succeed, and give yourself permission to

I CAN'T HEAR YOU DEAR!

succeed, then there is a good chance that you will. If you convince yourself that you are going to fail, then even if the circumstances are favourable, there is a good chance that you will fail in your endeavours.

You need to think about whether or not you are setting up the conditions which will allow you to achieve sound work–life balance. Are you setting up success or preparing to fail? Consider the following questions to help you to decide.

- Will you seek out success or be satisfied with achievements in life?
- How good are you at letting go of whatever stands in the way of your work–life balance aspirations?
- Do you value yourself enough to achieve sound work–life balance?
- Does guilt prevent you from achieving the work–life balance you are looking for?
- Do you look after your own health and wellbeing sufficiently well to allow you to achieve the work–life balance you want?

Success v achievement

Thinking about the differences between success and achievement is a variation on the 'I can do that' theme in the previous chapter. It also has relevance in your life outside work.

You noted when you worked through Chapter 3 that as a talented person you are capable of achieving a great deal. Remember that you achieve when you complete tasks successfully. An achievement could be something as simple as making sure that your register is taken on time every day or that you have enough food in the house to feed everyone over the weekend.

Success is something rather more personal. We value our successes so we could define our successes as the achievements which mean a lot to us. We remember our successes and would like to be remembered because of them. We all want more successes in our lives.

So the important question is: Do you allow yourself to succeed at what's important to you?

If your days are spent firefighting, or keeping the pot boiling, or working to keep the plates in the air, then you are an achiever. In some cases you will also consider this a success. You keep things going when others could not and are proud of what you are doing. But in the end, firefighting resolves nothing. You may be preventing a disaster but you are not remedying a bad situation when you are firefighting. You are also using your time – that finite and precious resource – on activities that are not really important to you.

Many people who give their lives over to achievements rather than to successes spend their lives dreaming about what they really want to do while taking no action towards fulfilling their aspirations. They anticipate what they are going to do at some point in the future: when their children have grown up, when they have that new job, when they have retired, when they have more money, when they have more time.

Many of those people find that they run out of life, or health, before they allow themselves to focus on their aspirations. Maybe something in the environment changes which takes away the opportunity to succeed. Maybe an illness gets in the way of their dreams. Maybe someone stops waiting for them to make that change, to fulfil their dreams. Whatever the reason, they fail to do whatever it is that they claim is important because they never allow themselves a chance to act. In the end their lives become filled with 'if onlys'.

If you wish to find the right work–life balance for you, make sure you focus on succeeding and not making do with present day, transitory achievements.

How good are you at letting go?

Whether you're thinking about aspects of your job, your relationship, the clothes in your wardrobe, a hobby or too many papers in your filing system at home or at work, just how good are you at letting go, at removing from your life what no longer serves the purpose it once did?

If you are going to get control of your life, and achieve the work–life balance you are looking for, you will need to remove some things from your life – at work and outside work – to allow yourself to make room for new tasks, activities, relationships, interests etc.

It is often easier to let go in school than it is elsewhere because a change of syllabus means that some teaching material becomes redundant, and your school probably has a policy about discarding old equipment and out-of-date resources when newer items arrive. It's not always so easy in your life outside work to let go of the past but it is something you need to do.

Think carefully about how you manage your life at present. Do you carry on as you always have, even though you know you are dissatisfied with the situation your actions are producing? If you do it may be time for some hard thinking. Only you will know when the time has come to let go, but you need a strategy that makes sure you do not settle for second best in life because you don't want to let go of what you no longer value or because taking action is just too difficult.

Do you value yourself enough to achieve work–life balance?

Having worked this far through the guide are you making progress with achieving the work–life balance you have been looking for? Are you making the progress you hoped you would be?

If you are struggling then ask where you stand in the prioritisation pecking order.

TRA-LA-LA...   NO-ONE HERE!

Do you always put yourself and your needs last? If you do, then no wonder that you are struggling to achieve the work–life balance you want because you are not allocating sufficient resource to the task.

Are you prepared to allocate time and energy to fulfilling your own work–life balance aspirations? Be honest when you reply because the question is essentially about your sense of self-worth and self-esteem.

If you do not value yourself you will never be able to justify prioritising what you want to do above the demands of others. If you always decide to put others' needs, demands and expectations before you own, whether you are dealing with your working life or with your life outside work, then there will never be time for what you want to do with your life. Therefore:

- Make sure you demonstrate you value your own work–life balance aspirations by allocating time to fulfil them.
- Make sure that despite your commitments to others you do not neglect your commitment to yourself.

Guilty as charged

Do you have a strong sense of what you *should* be doing with your time and how you *ought* to behave? If you have begun to allow yourself time to progress your work–life balance aspirations, do you feel guilty about all the other things you *should* have done while you were focusing on yourself?

If you feel guilty about taking time for yourself, then you have not as yet given yourself permission to succeed with your work–life balance.

Think carefully about the causes of your guilt. Sometimes the causes will not be well founded. For example, as a teacher you know you will never complete everything on your 'to do' list because in your job there are always new challenges and unmet needs. You need to accept this and allow yourself to take a break from working without feeling guilty about what you are not doing.

Remember also that if you are not using absolutely all your time to achieve something, there is no need to feel guilty. There are no rules that say you must use every waking minute productively. You are allowed time off. Time doing nothing is often essential to recharging your personal batteries.

As you work on your work–life balance, challenge that feeling of guilt, because it is almost certainly holding you back.

Keeping going

We all live busy lives in a busy world. With not enough time at work and little or no time outside work that is not assigned to dealingwith a range of responsibilities dictated by others or by your sense of what you should be doing, and squeezing in a little time here and there for yourself, you are almost certainly putting your health at risk.

If you do not exercise, do not eat properly, do not take time to slow down and relax then your lifestyle, over time, will almost certainly cause you problems. This will prevent you from doing what you think you ought to be doing, let alone achieving work–life balance. Strokes, cancers, heart attacks and other serious illnesses force people to slow down, sometimes permanently.

To preserve your health you need to make time to unwind. You need time to relax. You need to find a way to promote your own health and well-being. If time is a finite resource, so too are other things. Your health will not last forever. You will find that exhaustion creeps up on you. If you do not act, you will find yourself unhappy, unhealthy, unfit and unable to cope with many of the responsibilities you wish to fulfil both in your working life and in your life outside work.

If, as you are reading this chapter, you are telling yourself that you cannot afford the luxury of work–life balance or relaxation or time for yourself, then you urgently need to review your lifestyle.

- Make sure you put time for important self-maintenance into your schedule and be ruthless about protecting that time.

Think about the actions you take to maintain your health as deposits in the bank. This is one of the ways you build up your resource and your ability to cope with the demands that you face, so in anyone's terms it is a good investment.

Towards work–life balance

This is the point in the guide where you will start to move rapidly towards your work–life balance goals.

Now that you have dealt with what can get in the way of your work–life balance, both in your working life and in your life outside work, you can begin to think about what sort of life you want and plan to achieve it. You will then be able to decide on the relationship you wish to create between your working life and your life outside work – your work–life balance.

But isn't work–life balance just about good time management?

No, it is not. Many people in all walks of life believe that work–life balance is just about applying the disciplines of time management to all parts of their lives. Such people strive to be as organised in their personal lives as they have learned to be at work. They prioritise systematically and they delegate ruthlessly. They make appointments to spend time with friends and family and they diarise social activities to make sure they do not get squeezed out of their schedules.

People who are good at time management fit lots of tasks and activities into their schedules at work and in their lives outside work. If most people struggle to juggle with seven balls, they keep eleven aloft with ease. Their juggling ability, the ability to keep many pots boiling, is a major source of their success in managing their lives.

You can learn a lot from these people, and remember, if you are to stand even a remote chance of achieving the right work–life balance for you, you will need to develop excellent time management skills.

But do not fall into the trap of thinking that work–life balance is just about time management. Successful time management does not necessarily result in your being able to lead the life you want to lead, and therefore it does not necessarily lead to sound work–life balance. If the time you make by developing your time management skills and containing work within defined limits is just then used to allow you to complete a range of different and additional tasks in your life outside work, can you really call this achieving work–life balance?

SURELY THIS ISNT WORK-LIFE BALANCE!

Successful time management will help you to create more discretionary time – time which is yours to allocate as you wish. Your aim with all your time management activities is to create more discretionary time in your life.

Do you know what you want out of life?

Containing work is just a holding action; self-maintenance is a necessity for survival. All of the tactics noted above will help you to create time for you to use as you wish. Now think about why you want that discretionary time and how you intend to use it.

More important than any of the above is the question about what you want from your life – both in your working life and in your life outside work – and that must be the focus of your attention now.

However, you may find it difficult to think about what you really want. You haven't done this very often in the past; you have never had the time. Now, as you begin to ask yourself the question, maybe you find you don't know the answer.

Whether or not you find yourself in that situation it is worth reviewing your life planning process in the context of the emotional commitments you make in all components of your life. This will give you an insight into what you really want out of life.

Emotional commitments

As a teacher you make an emotional commitment to your job. You work in what has often been called a 'caring profession'. You find it difficult to walk away from your work at the end of the day because you care about people. You care about your family and your friends too, and you make emotional commitments to them. You may also have made a strong emotional commitment to things in which you believe passionately or to an all-consuming interest.

What you believe in and what you value are strong indictors of where your emotional commitments lie.

- Identifying your strongest emotional commitment is what helps you to decide what you value right now and what's important to you.

You will have made emotional commitments to people, to aspects of your work, to your beliefs, to almost anything that matters to you.

- Anything to which you have made an emotional commitment is something which is important to you.
- Anyone to whom you have made an emotional commitment is important to you.

Now think about your life in terms of how you manage your emotional commitments in the different areas of your life, not in terms of how you manage your time.

- Your successes in life, as opposed to your achievements, are almost always linked to your emotional commitments.

Reviewing your emotional commitments will help you with all aspects of life planning and with your aspiration to achieve sound work–life balance.

Activity 4.1, which is at the end of the chapter, deals with what you want to fit into your life and the emotional commitments you make to all your activities.

Complete the activity now if you would like to reflect on your emotional commitments immediately. Complete it when you have finished reading the chapter if you would prefer to do all the activities together.

If you have poor work–life balance, and if you are dissatisfied with aspects of your life, there is a good chance that your analysis will show that you do not allocate your time in accordance with your emotional commitments.

Once you have completed the activity you will know where to focus your efforts.

Getting work–life balance right

Achieving work–life balance is first about making sure the major components of your life are filled with activities and relationships which you value and then about managing the relationship between these components effectively.

You now need to ensure that you allocate any discretionary time you are able to create to what is important to you.

In the short term you are adjusting how you allocate your discretionary time and making sure your allocations better reflect your emotional commitments. In the longer term you will need to think about adjusting your life in more far-reaching ways to ensure that more of your time is allocated to activities to which you have made a strong emotional commitment.

Aim to ensure that the principal activities in your life are geared towards helping you to succeed in what is important to you.

Managing constraints

You cannot necessarily do exactly what you want to do right now and achieve exactly the right work–life balance today. As you plan your work–life balance journey, think about the constraints that affect your ability to achieve your goals and plan to minimise their impact on your plans.

Constraints on your actions could include those linked to:

- Health – poor health can limit your ambitions, but people who are not in perfect health can achieve great things too.
- Personal circumstances – if you have built up a large amount of personal debt you may need to take action to pay it off before you can take time out to study, take up a job in a more expensive location or take a job with less responsibility to allow you to focus more on activities outside work.
- The needs of others – your emotional commitments may mean that you are prioritising your children's needs or the needs of other relatives or close friends over your own at present, but children grow up and other relationships change, so these are finite commitments.

Constraints do not necessarily prevent you from fulfilling your work–life balance plans; you just need to take them into account and minimise their ability to get in your way.

The work–life balancing act

Once your actions in your working life and your life outside work reflect what you want in life, the final aspect of achieving the work–life balance you have been looking for will be deciding where you wish to place the boundary between your working life and the rest of your life. This is not as easy as it sounds.

You will have different aspirations in your twenties from those you nurture in your forties. Your aspirations in your sixties will be different again. In your twenties you may prioritise work, and set yourself the task of becoming a good teacher as your key objective. In your thirties you might hanker after more authority and responsibility, maybe by becoming a deputy head teacher or a head teacher. In your forties, perhaps you find you have too much of both. In your sixties – and for an increasing number of teachers these will continue to be years spent at work – you might have aspirations you do not even imagine in your thirties.

Your life outside work could have great importance to you at any time in your working life, whether you have a responsibility for raising children, for taking care of your partner, for helping elderly relatives or a consuming interest to which you would like to devote more time. These issues all affect your decision about where you want to place the boundary between your working life and your life outside work.

Part of the life planning and work–life balance challenge is that of remaining aware of what is important to you – remaining aware of where your emotional commitments lie – and adjusting your life to make sure your time allocations reflect what is important to you. When doing this remember:

- You are also allowed to change your mind.
- Your needs and wants can and do change.
- If you get something wrong with your plan you're allowed to try something different.

You will know you have achieved the right work–life balance for you, you will know when you have reached your work–life balance destination, when your answer to the question: 'What sort of life do I want to lead?' is 'The sort of life I have now'.

Even when you have finished working with this guide ask yourself this question regularly.

If, having read this chapter you think you need more guidance on issues raised here, you will find that a great deal has been written about personal effectiveness, motivation, assertiveness, self-confidence, self-esteem and related issues. Use this literature to help you to take control of your whole life. Remember that you are trying to create a situation where your answers to the question about the life you want to lead is always 'the sort of life I have now'.

Now that you have finished reading this chapter complete activity 4.2, which looks at the work–life balance decisions some teachers have made. If you have not completed activity 4.1 do that activity at this stage too.

Summary – key points

1 This section of the guide looks at ways of helping your gain more control over your life outside work.

2 It will also help you to be clear on what you want out of life, to define the work–life balance you are looking for and to decide where you wish to set the boundaries between your working life and your life outside work.

3 To achieve your goal you will need to create more discretionary time. Discretionary time is the raw material of your work–life balance successes.

4 You will need to apply your learning from Chapter 3 as many of the issues you face in your life outside work will be similar to those you encounter at work. For example, you will need to learn not to be too responsive to others and to understand the differences between busy and effective in your life outside work, just as you did when you reviewed your working life.

5 In order to attain the work–life balance you are looking for you will need to focus on success rather than on achievements, let go of what stands in the way of your work–life balance aspirations, value yourself enough to allow yourself to achieve work–life balance, avoid allowing guilt to prevent you from taking action to achieve work–life balance and make sure that you do not neglect your health.

6 You will also need to develop excellent time management skills.

7 In order to help you to establish what you want in life review your emotional commitments.

8 Use your discretionary time to address those things to which you have made an emotional commitment because what is important to you in life is almost always linked to your emotional commitments.

9 For the future try to make sure that your principal activities are geared towards helping you to succeed in what is important to you.

10 Take constraints into account but take action to minimise their impact on your work–life balance plans.

11 Think about where you wish to place the boundary between your working life and your life outside work and acknowledge that you will place that boundary in different places at different points in your life.

Activities

These activities will help you to take control of your life outside work and to find the right work–life balance for you. Activity 4.2 is particularly suitable for use in a school-based staff development session.

Look at the list of possible components of your life and decide which activities you would like to place under each heading. Include at least five activities you would like to fit into each part of your life under each heading.

If you wish to change the headings, or add to the list, do so.

Components of your life	Column A	Column B
	Emotional commitment	More or less (+ or −)
Working life (e.g. marking, teaching, keeping up to date)		
Social life (e.g. having time to spend with friends, to go out with friends)		
Responsibilities outside work – tasks which are not also hobbies (e.g. household maintenance, car fixing etc.)		

Responsibilities outside work – to others (e.g. responsibility for the upbringing of children, caring and support responsibilities)		
Hobbies and interests		
Relationships (taking time to build and sustain relationships with people who matter to you)		
Other		

Now revisit the list you have made of what is important to you and allocate an emotional commitment rating of between one and ten to each activity. Note these ratings in column A.

Minimal emotional commitment   Strong emotional commitment

1	2	3	4	5	6	7	8	9	10

If you have more than one activity in any component of your life where you have awarded a rating of 10, try to decide which is the more important activity and give that a 10-plus rating.

Highlight the activity and rating in each component of your life which has the *highest* rating.

Then complete column B using plus or minus signs to indicate if you think you need to allocate more or less time to that activity in order to ensure that the time you spend on it reflects its importance in your life and your emotional commitment to it.

Now highlight the activity and rating in each component of your life which has the *lowest* rating. Do you need to spend more or less time on this activity?

Overall, does your allocation of time to activities reflect their importance to you? If the answer is yes, then you are well on the way to achieving the right work–life balance for you. If not, how could you use your discretionary time – that is the time that you have created through the careful management of your life – to make sure your allocations of time reflect more appropriately your emotional commitments and what is important in your life?

Note your responses below.

ACTIVITY 4.2: MANAGING YOUR LIFE

This activity deals with three teachers who are working hard to achieve the right work–life balance for them. Have a look at what they are saying about themselves and their work–life balance and then consider the questions which follow.

Paul, a head of department in a comprehensive school, age 32

'My head teacher wants me to go on a three-day training course next month. It's about preparing for deputy headship and it's run by a very well-known national training organisation. Unfortunately, it's a long way away and if I went I'd have to spend three nights away from home.

'I've explained to the head that I can't go and that didn't go down too well. I am committed to my job and I do want to be a deputy, but I'm not going on that course.

'My daughter gets upset when I'm away. She doesn't like it if I'm not there at night. My wife says she'd get over it – and maybe she would – but I don't really want her to find out she can manage without me, not at her age anyway. I'm not going. My mind's made up.'

If you were Paul, how would you explain to your colleagues and to your head teacher that you take your career seriously but you also take your responsibilities as a parent seriously.

Mel, a teacher with four years' experience in a primary school, age 29

'I am ambitious and I don't care who knows it. I will be a head in a small school within five years, and I'll have another headship pretty quickly after that.

'I'm doing a master's degree in my spare time. It's a gruelling pace. No time for nights down the pub or holidays for a couple of years for me. My time's fully booked.

'It's a distance learning programme so I didn't have to ask to have any time out of school. I have four weekend sessions and a summer school to attend during the year and plenty of assignments.

'I think it's worth it. I've already taken on more responsibility in school thanks to my course, and although that means I have even less time than I anticipated for anything else I'm getting where I want to go and that's what matters to me.'

If you were Mel, how would you explain your current approach to your life to your family and friends?

Jas, a teacher with ten years' experience in a comprehensive school, age 43

'I used to play competitively. I've got lots of medals and awards, and polish them every week. I've never let my interest lag. Every weekend I'm out there refereeing and coaching. I've got all the coaching certificates too, over the years.

'I'm glad I teach the game for a few lessons a week. It's a shame that I didn't train as a PE teacher when I was younger.

'Anyway, things are going to change now. I have been asked to referee on the international circuit and that'll mean time out of school during term time. A trip to Australia is coming up this winter.

'I can't afford to give up teaching. The money for the refereeing's fine, but it's not a full-time job. I'm hoping the head will find a way to let me stay in the school and still go and do my refereeing. It will give the school some good publicity, and I keep saying I'm happy to do more sports teaching when I'm here. I've got to go and see the head this afternoon. I hope he's as excited about my news as I am.'

If you were Jas, how would you explain to your head teacher that it's the right decision to try to find a way to help you to stay on the staff and take up the refereeing opportunity?

CHAPTER 5

The new working environment

As you have worked through this guide you have focused to a very great extent on work–life balance with reference to yourself and your school life, but the world is a much bigger place than that, and a lot is happening out there that will help you with your journey towards achieving sound work–life balance.

Some of the developments are taking place in the world of education; some are taking place in the world of work more generally and, in turn, influencing education. You need to be aware of them so that you know what type of support is available to help you to achieve your work–life balance aspirations.

This chapter will also help you to find the right way to promote work–life balance to senior people in your school.

Work–life balance at work

Work–life balance and the world of work

Work–life balance has a place in the world of work. The term itself is an excellent sound bite, so you hear it a lot, but as you already know, it is used in very different ways. Chapter 1 showed how employers and individuals tend to define and use the term. Government is also involved with the work–life balance agenda.

Government aims to use the work–life balance agenda among other things to:

- remove barriers to employment
- help people to get work and stay in work.

There are numerous entitlements, introduced recently, for people responsible for the upbringing of children. For example, the 2002 Employment Act gives those with responsibility for the upbringing of children under the age or 6 or those with responsibility for the upbringing of a child with disabilities under the age of 18 the right to request to work flexibly and to have that request considered seriously. There are limited grounds on which an employer can refuse such requests. Employees whose requests are refused have recourse to an employment tribunal.

Other recent developments deal with maternity and parental leave, and paternity and adoption leave. Such developments are of interest to you as a teacher because legislation, relevant directives and good practice guides are all helping to change the ways in which everyone's work is organised. Teachers, like other members of the workforce, may wish to consider taking advantage of these arrangements to help them to achieve the right work–life balance for them.

While you will have your own reasons for promoting work–life balance in your school, you are likely to find senior people are more interested in work–life balance if you find ways of also demonstrating that:

- work–life balance can help schools to raise standards and improve their performance
- people management problems faced by your school can be addressed at least in part via the work–life balance agenda.

Much of the literature surrounding work–life balance demonstrates that this agenda can help organisations to improve their performance and be more successful, for example in helping them to deal with a range of people management problems including:

- staff recruitment
- staff retention and turnover

- high levels of absenteeism
- poor staff morale
- low levels of overall productivity/poor standards of performance.

You may find it helpful to read up about some of these developments. Use the bibliography in this guide as your starting point.

Work–life balance strategies

There are numerous work–life balance strategies in use today. These are the means by which the work–life balance agenda is implemented and they deal primarily with new ways of organising and managing work. The strategies used most often are:

- flexible working arrangements
- work breaks
- child care and adult care provision
- employee facilities and other provisions.

Flexible working arrangements, which are widely used work–life strategies, include:

- **annualised hours** – calculating the total number of hours to be worked in a year and then distributing working time in a range of ways throughout the working year
- **part-time working** – working any combination of hours which is less than full-time
- **job-sharing** – splitting the responsibilities of one job between two people
- **home working/remote working** – working for part of the working week at home or at another location
- **voluntary reduced time (v-time)** – employees reduce the number of hours they work but lose pay. They retain the right to return to full-time hours
- **the non-standard working week** or the compressed or consolidated working week – working the normal hours for the job over four days

instead of five, or a nine day fortnight or working longer or shorter weeks at different times of the year

- **flexi-time** – there are core working times when people must be at work but outside that core time people choose when they start and finish work and take their breaks
- **time off in lieu** – a *quid pro quo* arrangement which allows people to take time off to compensate for hours they have worked in addition to their contracted hours.

Flexible working does not necessarily mean working part-time. In many cases flexible working means that full-time hours are worked in different ways and at different locations.

Work breaks occur when someone takes time out from his or her job but can return to that same job. The length of a work break is usually defined: one year, one term etc. Work breaks are often unpaid. Sabbatical leave is a form of work break which may or may not be paid leave. Study leave or leave to allow someone to take up public service of community responsibilities or leave to compete in sporting events would also be classed as work breaks.

Childcare and adult care arrangements support employees who have caring responsibilities outside their working lives. Recent legislation gives working parents and adopters particular rights (see above) and it is in this area that there is the largest growth in the take up of work–life balance arrangements. Employers often choose to help their employees to manage other caring responsibilities in order to ensure they do not lose people's expertise. Some employers offer extended leave beyond the legally specified limits. They offer childcare allowances. They offer 'sick child' leave. A fast-growing area of support for employees is related to eldercare, that is support to help people to care for elderly relatives.

Employee facilities and other provisions include Employee Assistance Programmes (EAP) and the majority of employee wellbeing programmes. EAP often include stress and debt counselling support and 'hot lines' to help people to deal with bereavements, drugs, alcohol and other problems. Wellbeing programmes aim to promote healthy lifestyles and to create healthy working environments. These may include keep fit classes, use of gym facilities etc.

I ASKED ABOUT WORKING FLEXIBLY AND
THE HEAD GAVE ME THIS BOOK ON YOGA

But surely this won't work in education?

Education has already made some significant progress with a range of initiatives which support teachers' efforts to improve their work–life balance. These are excellent developments and can all help teachers on their work–life balance journey. They include moves to:

- reduce the number of activities unrelated to teaching and learning which are completed by teachers
- take teachers' wellbeing into account as part of school leadership responsibilities
- increase the number of support staff in schools to take on the jobs which teachers have relinquished
- encourage teachers to focus their efforts on teaching and learning and on the management of the curriculum.

Teachers are beginning to take up some of the options available to them under the terms of recent legislation, including adopting flexible working. Therefore, when thinking about work–life balance, you need to remember that just as with the rest of the world of employment, working practices in education are changing.

Although schools may prefer to have the same teacher on site each day and every day, in some cases that may no longer be possible. If there are not enough people willing to take teaching jobs on these terms, then schools, like other organisations, will be obliged to:

- change the ways in which they organise work
- adopt more flexible approaches to employment
- utilise a range of different attendance patterns for their staff.

Activity 5.1, which you will find at the end of the chapter, asks you to think about how some of the work–life balance strategies dealt with in this chapter can help you and your school.

Complete the activity now if you would like to reflect on work–life balance strategies and related issues immediately. Complete it when you have finished reading the chapter if you would prefer to do all the activities together.

Standards and benchmarks

External benchmarks are always helpful when promoting changes to working practices. You may find it helpful in terms of your own work–life balance and in terms of helping your school, to make sure your head teacher and governing body are aware of some of the standards and benchmarks which promote good practice in the field of people management. These include the following:

- The Investors in People Work–Life Balance Model, which was launched in 2003, provides an assessment framework and good practice development model covering the key work–life balance issues, including making sure the culture of the organisation supports work–life balance.
- The Health and Safety Executive's standards, which are designed to help organisations to improve continuously how they tackle work-related stress, focus on six key areas. These are: the demands made on employees; the level of control employees have over their work; the support they receive; the clarity of their roles; the nature of relationships at work; and how change is managed.
- Contests to find the 'best' organisations in particular categories, which are promoted via a range of organisations also draw attention, among

other things, to work–life balance issues. The *Sunday Times* publishes its list of 100 best companies to work for each year. The Great Place to Work® Institute UK publishes The Best Workplaces list annually. Contest results, as well as offering a ranking of successful organisations, also offer guidance on what successful organisations do to merit their designation as 'best'.

Promoting work–life balance in your school

Now that you have done so much work on your own work–life balance, the time has come for you to decide how best to promote work–life balance to the senior people in your school.

If your school takes work–life balance seriously then everything you are trying to achieve in terms of your personal work–life balance will be that much easier. That in itself is a good reason for considering using the following approaches in school:

1   Raise awareness of the whole work–life balance agenda and the benefits it can deliver to organisations and to individuals. As part of this process think about letting your school know about the Health and Safety Executive's Stress Management Standards or the Investors in People Work–Life Balance Model or the contests which lead to the identification of 'best' organisations.

2   Look at the people management problems your school is facing: recruitment, retention, poor morale etc. Explain to senior people how implementing the work–life balance agenda can help with all of these problems.

3   Suggest that your school develops a work–life balance policy. This may be a separate, stand-alone policy. It might be part of your health and safety policy. You might develop a stress management policy and a work–life balance policy separately; it doesn't really matter. What is important is to get other people involved, and the development of a policy is a good way of doing this, provided that, as part of the process, you make sure that people understand what work–life balance is and why it matters in school.

4   During the policy-making process get people to think about which work–life balance strategies your school is going to support. In the interests of fairness and equality state what they are, who will be

eligible to apply, how they should apply and the criteria to be used to judge their applications.

5   Make sure that senior staff and everyone with a leadership role understands the current legislation and how adopting work–life balance strategies in school will affect the way they work. It is no use, for example, implementing a homeworking policy if a head of key stage or head of department has a habit of calling meetings on an *ad hoc* basis and demanding everyone's attendance.

6   Make sure that the group developing the policy and work–life balance provisions also takes responsibility for promoting their adoption to the senior team and governing body.

7   Set up a troubleshooting group to deal with implementation problems and to be responsible for the ongoing monitoring and review of how work–life balance is working in your school.

8   Decide how you are going to measure the benefits of your work–life balance activities both for individuals and for your school.

Now that you have finished reading this chapter complete activity 5.2 which re-introduces you to someone you already know who is struggling to find the right work–life balance.

If you have not already completed activity 5.1, do that activity at this stage too.

As you move to the final chapter of the guide, armed with guidance to help you to achieve sound work–life balance for yourself and with ideas about how best to promote work–life balance in your school, you need to think about pulling together all you have learned into a coherent, long-term work–life balance strategy.

This is an important task, as you will be applying this strategy for as long as you are at work.

Summary – key points

1   This chapter looks at work–life balance developments in the world of work.

2 Recent legislation and other developments mean that some people in work have the right to ask to work flexibly and to have their requests considered seriously. There are also extended leave arrangements for parents and for those adopting children.

3 Work–life balance strategies fall into four main categories: flexible working; career breaks; childcare and adult care provision; and employee facilities and other provisions. Flexible working strategies are very widely used.

4 Teachers need to be aware of these developments because they affect how work is organised, employment options and patterns of attendance at work.

5 When teachers promote the work–life balance agenda in their schools they need to ensure they explain how their proposals help individuals and their school.

6 A strategy for promoting work–life balance in schools is outlined in this chapter.

Activities

These activities will help you to place work–life balance in the broader working context and to be more aware of how you and others can use the range of work–life balance strategies in school.

Both activities are suitable for use in school-based staff development sessions.

ACTIVITY 5.1: WORKING FLEXIBLY

Use this activity to help you to establish the benefits of flexible working for you and for your school.

Look again at the work–life balance strategies listed in this chapter. They fall into four main categories:

- flexible working arrangements
- work breaks
- childcare and adult care provision
- employee facilities and other provisions.

Identify three actions linked to any of these categories you think would help people in your school to fulfil their work–life balance aspirations, e.g. *If our school offered us a healthy living programme the value of taking exercise and eating properly would have a higher priority with us*.

1

2

3

Now consider flexible working in more detail. The main flexible working strategies are:

- annualised hours
- part-time working
- job-sharing
- home working/remote working
- voluntary reduced time (v-time)
- the non-standard working week
- flexi-time
- time off in lieu.

How would you promote the benefits of flexible working to your head teacher/your senior team/your governing body? Identify two important reasons why your school should be promoting flexible working.

1

2

Which of these flexible working options could help you to fulfil your own work–life balance aspirations? Tick the relevant options. Note the two you are most likely to wish to take up and identify a reason why your decision would be beneficial to you and to your school.

First work–life balance strategy:
My reason:

Supporting my school:

Second work–life balance strategy:
My reason:

Supporting my school:

Looking ahead, say three to five years, do you think you would wish to use any of the work–life balance strategies mentioned in this chapter at that time to help you to achieve sound work–life balance?

ACTIVITY 5.2: FINDING A SOLUTION

This activity asks you to find a way of helping Jas, the teacher you met in Activity 4.2, with his work–life balance decisions.

As you enter the staff room Jas looks up from polishing a sports trophy. He has a selection of his medals, cups and other awards on the table in front of him. Everything is shiny and spotless. You can see that Jas takes great pride in his sporting achievements. As you approach, he beams at you and says 'I'm glad you've come. I have a lot to think about so I'm glad I'm able to talk things through with you. I saw the head this afternoon about my refereeing trips. You know that, of course, that's why you're here.

'The head didn't know how much I have done for the sport. He said he knew I used to play but he hadn't seen the medals and the like. He asked me if I had ever thought about teaching PE. I was flabbergasted.

'I explained to him about the offers I have to referee abroad on two major tours in the next academic year.

'He started off by offering me a career break – a year off without pay and the right to come back to my existing job. He said it would make it easiest for the school to find a replacement if I took a whole year off. I had to tell him straight away that I couldn't afford that option.

'I will be paid when I'm on the two trips – Australia in November and December; home for Christmas; and the Pacific tour in April and May; but that leaves a lot of time when I won't be earning. I told the head I have a mortgage and I have to pay something to my ex-wife towards the upbringing of our son. I told him I had already thought about supply work for the rest of the time, but it's a bit risky. I need a regular income.

'The head then said that perhaps I should take the career break and do some supply work here. The head of PE is waiting for a date to go into hospital for an operation on his knee, so they will need someone to fill in. Trouble is, the operation might come at a time when I'm on one of the trips.

'We also talked about my going part-time for a year and doing more hours in some parts of the year than in others. I don't know about that. That's one of the things I need to talk to you about. I don't know how that would work. The head said he wouldn't need me at all in June or July because of the exams.

'The head also said I should speak to someone about how all of this will affect my pension.

'At the end of the interview I mentioned the Olympics and my hope of refereeing there. The head asked me about my long-term plans as soon as I raised that subject. Will I just be away for these two trips or are we talking about a long-term rearrangement of my working life?

'I looked blank when he asked. I wish I knew the answer.'

When Jas stops speaking and looks at you expectantly, what are you going to say?

How can you help both Jas and his school?

Possible answer:
The key here is to keep as many options open for Jas as possible. He hasn't made up his mind about his long-term plans so he needs more time before he thinks about giving up his job. Whether or not he adopts a part-time working pattern for the coming year, this will only address part of the issue. However, there probably is a solution around annualised hours, part-time working or v-time.

The head may have a need for Jas's expertise during the year so there is something to build on here. The school has an opportunity to use the expertise of someone who is in the international class as far as his sport is concerned. Schools try hard to get such people to come and support them. This is one such person readily available if the school can find the right way to secure his expertise.

The main constraints on Jas are financial, so you will need to advise him to do some serious financial planning and take advice from experts about his options. The head teacher was also right to suggest Jas review how his pension will be affected by his decisions. You should endorse this recommendation.

CHAPTER 6

Can you achieve work–life balance and stay in teaching?

Overview

This chapter will help you to draw together the actions you need to take to ensure that having achieved work–life balance you are able to hold onto it.

Introduction

Whatever you thought when you began working through this guide, by now you know that staying in teaching and achieving the work–life balance you are looking for is possible.

You know you can't do it alone. You can't achieve sound work–life balance just as a result of your own efforts; your school also needs to take work–life balance seriously if you are going to succeed.

You also know that your school can't do it for you. Only you can achieve the work–life balance you are looking for; only you will know when you have achieved it; only you can take control of your working life and manage your life outside work so that you can set the boundary between these two important components of your life in the place that is right for you. Only you will know when your work–life balance aspirations change and when you need to change your work–life balance plan.

Taking stock – where are you now?

By now you have achieved a lot in terms of your work–life balance. Recognise your achievements and congratulate yourself on what you have done.

Now look again at the work–life balance audit. Complete it a second time and compare the results with those you achieved when you first worked through the activity.

- What new information does completing the audit a second time offer you?
- Have your scores improved?
- Have you identified different development areas this time?

Whatever you have achieved and whatever you still need to do, now is the time to be vigilant. Your job is one that makes enormous demands on you intellectually, physically and emotionally. It will always be a battle to ensure it does not demand too much of your life.

Sustaining your work–life balance will remain a difficult balancing act for you, especially as your aspirations for your work and your work–life balance will change over time. Work will be more or less important to you at different points in your life.

Make sure you continue to contain your work within the limits that are right for you now.

Continue to use Chapter 3 to keep you on track. Revisit activities 3.1 and 3.2 from time to time.

You will also need to remember that work–life balance is not just about keeping your working life in check. Reconsider on a regular basis what you want out of your life and what work–life balance you are looking for.

Don't forget boundary management activities. Where do you want to draw the line between your working life and your life outside work? Work–life balance will not be yours if you are forever trying to squeeze more and more into each component of your life. Something will give and in the long run that will be you.

Use Chapter 4 to help you to decide what you want out of life, what work–life balance is right for you and where to establish the boundary between your working life and your life outside work. Revisit activity 4.1 from time to time.

However, the best piece of advice you can give yourself is to avoid becoming too caught up in your own situation. The world of work is changing, and changing rapidly. It will continue to change and you need to keep up to date with what is happening to ensure you help yourself and your school to make the best use of available work–life balance support processes.

Use Chapter 5 of the guide to remind you of the range of support mechanisms and continue to read about developments to the work–life balance agenda. Revisit activity 5.1 from time to time.

Your work–life balance plan

Finally, you need a plan, a means of keeping yourself on track. Use it to make sure that you do not lose the work–life balance you have worked so hard to achieve.

Make a copy of the prompts which follow and use them to help you to continue on your work–life balance journey:

1 Be clear about what sound work–life balance means to you right now.
2 Be clear on what you want in terms of work–life balance.
3 Ensure that you keep control of your working life.
4 Ensure that you give yourself permission to work towards the work–life balance you are looking for.
5 Be clear about where you wish to set the boundary between your working life and your life outside work.
6 Learn how to let go of anything that is holding you back.
7 Take advantage of external sources of support to help you to achieve your work–life balance aspirations.
8 Make sure you accept that your work–life balance aspirations will change.
9 Revise and update your work–life balance strategy regularly.
10 Follow the guidance – no excuses.

Now that you are in charge of your work–life balance journey, enjoy it!

Summary – key points

1 This section draws together what you have learned as you have worked through the guide into a coherent lifelong work–life balance strategy.

2 It outlines what you need to do now to sustain the work–life balance you have worked so hard to achieve.

3 Revisit some of the activities in the guide from time to time.

4 Produce a plan that will help you to keep on track with your work–life balance.

Bibliography

Further reading

Changing Times – A TUC Guide to Work–Life Balance
Trades Union Congress (2001)

First Things First
Stephen R. Covey, A. Roger Merrill and Rebecca R. Merrill
Simon and Schuster (1994)

Flexible Working
John Stredwick and Steve Ellis
Chartered Institute of Personnel and Development (CIPD) (2005)

Stress at Work
Health and Safety Executive/ACAS (2004)

The Teleworking Handbook (4th edition)
Alan Denbigh
A & C Black (2003)

Wellness at Work – Promoting and Protecting Employee Wellbeing
Lynda A. C. MacDonald
Chartered Institute of Personnel and Development (CIPD) (2005)

The Work–Life Balance Model
Investors in People UK (2003)

The Work–Life Balance Trainer's Manual – Fifteen Ready-made Development Activities for Trainers
Margaret Adams
Gower Publishing Ltd (2003)

Websites

The following websites all contain information about work–life balance, wellbeing, work-related stress and similar themes which are regularly updated:

www.acas.org.uk
www.businesslink.gov.uk
www.cipd.co.uk
www.hse.gov.uk
www.investorsinpeople.co.uk
www.tuc.org.uk

Appendix: *Instant work–life balance?*

Try asking people in your staff room about their progress with work–life balance. Post these pages on your notice board.

How are you faring with the work–life balance challenge?

Are you keeping your head above water or are you struggling?

Here is an opportunity to try out ten questions from the Work–Life Balance Audit in Margaret Adams's book, *Work–Life Balance: A Practical Guide for Teachers* (published by David Fulton Publishers, 2006).

Complete these questions now to see how well you are doing with work–life balance:

1 What do you do when you have too much to do and too many calls on your time?

   a Try to do everything and so some things badly   ❑

   b Concentrate on the important things and let the others go   ❑

   c Do the things that people shout loudest to have done   ❑

2 On a day when everyone in school seems to be busy, several people are asking you to help them. Given that you cannot help everyone, in which order should you accept additional tasks?

     1 Tasks I like doing
     2 Tasks that only I can do
     3 Any tasks linked to my job
     4 asks where the deadline for completion is earliest

   a 1, 2, 3, 4   ❑

   b 2, 3, 4, 1   ❑

   c 2, 4, 1, 3   ❑

3 Do you often wake up in the night thinking about work?

   a Yes ❑

   b No ❑

4 Do you have hobbies and interests outside your work?

   a Yes ❑

   b No ❑

5 How often do you allocate a quiet time somewhere in your schedule (before school, after school, in non-contact time etc.) when you can reflect on your priorities?

   a At least once a week ❑

   b About once a month ❑

   c I never have time to be quiet ❑

6 The prime purpose of health and wellbeing programmes is:

   a To help people to improve their work–life balance ❑

   b To prevent illness and injury and to promote good health among all staff ❑

   c To help people who are not coping ❑

7 Which indicates the better use of time?

   a Doing the right thing ❑

   b Doing things right ❑

8 You want to take up a new activity (e.g. learn a foreign language, riding, cookery etc.) but just can't fit it into your current schedule. What do you say?

   a I'll have time for it, one day, maybe when I retire ❑

   b I'll stop doing something I do at present to make room ❑

   c It's not fair. Why can't I do what I want with my life? ❑

9 On a day when you are particularly busy a colleague asks you to take on an extra task. The first question you should ask yourself before taking on that task is:

   a Does the job need to be done? ❑

   b Can I do this job? ❑

   c Whose responsibility is the job? ❑

10 And finally, which of the following sums up your feelings about your own work–life balance?

  a I have achieved the right work–life balance for me ❏

  b One day I'll think about work–life balance. For the moment I've too much else to do ❏

  c I have made some changes to the way I work, but I need to do more ❏

For each right answer you score a point. You score no points for any other answer.

1	2	3	4	5	6	7	8	9	10
b	b	b	a	a	b	a	b	a	a

- If you got seven points or more, you will find some of what you are already doing is covered in the book because you are already on the right track. Use the book to help you to understand why you are successful and to achieve even better work–life balance.

- If you got between four and six points, then you are beginning to make progress but you need to give work–life balance a higher profile in your life. Look at Chapters 3 and 4 in *Work–Life Balance: A Practical Guide for Teachers* for ideas.

- If you got fewer than four points then start thinking about work–life balance now and use *Work–Life Balance: A Practical Guide for Teachers* to help you.

Index

abilities
   expertise 42
   feasibility and 40
   overestimating 54–5
achievement
   limitations 78
   success and 54–5, 73–74
   visibility and 45–6
adult care 93
after-school meetings 16–17
age 24, 82–3
annualised hours 92
aspirations
   age on 82
   success from 74
audit 18–36, 104
autonomy 101
   constraints on 5–6, 19–20
   unilateral action 50
awareness
   of new practices 89, 103
   raising 96

bank, teaching resource 17
belief
   on failure 73
   on success 72–3
benchmarks 95–6
'best' organisations 95–6
blame 38
busyness, effectiveness and 55–6

care provision
   adult care 93
   childcare 21, 91, 93
   eldercare 24, 93
caring 80
childcare 21, 93
   flexible working for 91
collaboration 53
commitment 76
   emotional 80, 82

compressed working week 91–2
constraints 81–2 *see also* individual terms
containment of work 69–70
costs, opportunity 25, 53–4

debt 82
delegation 44–5
discipline 69–70
   achievement from 78
discretionary time 68, 79, 81
distractions 24–5, 57

e-mail
   constraints from 18
   discipline on 69–70
EAPs (Employee Assistance Programmes) 93
effectiveness, busyness and 55–6
eldercare 24, 93
emotional commitment
   scope 80, 82
   success from 80
Employee Assistance Programmes (EAPs) 93
Employment Act 2002 16, 20, 91
enjoyment, workloads 4
entitlements
   care 21, 24, 91, 93
   leave 23–4, 91, 93
   on recruitment 90–1
esteem, self- 35, 76
exhaustion 72
expertise 42

failure, belief on 73
family 5
feasibility
   ability and 40
   scope 41
   support for 41–2
flexible working 16, 20
   accommodation to 95
   annualised hours 92
   for childcare 91